of destinations around the world, sharing with travellers a wealth of experience and a passion for travel.

Rely on Thomas Cook as your travelling companion on your next trip and benefit from our unique heritage.

Thomas Cook **pocket** guides

KRAKOW

Your travelling companion since 1873

Written by Richard Schofield, updated by Renata Rubnikowicz

Published by Thomas Cook Publishing
A division of Thomas Cook Tour Operations Limited
Company registration no. 3772199 England
The Thomas Cook Business Park, 9 Coningsby Road,
Peterborough PE3 8SB, United Kingdom
Email: books@thomascook.com, Tel: +44 (0) 1733 416477
www.thomascookpublishing.com

Produced by Cambridge Publishing Management Limited
Burr Elm Court, Main Street, Caldecote CB23 7NU
www.cambridgepm.co.uk

ISBN: 978-1-84848-433-7

© 2007, 2009 Thomas Cook Publishing
This third edition © 2011 Thomas Cook Publishing
Text © Thomas Cook Publishing
Maps © Thomas Cook Publishing/PCGraphics (UK) Limited
Transport map © Communicarta Limited

Series Editor: Karen Beaulah
Production/DTP: Steven Collins

Printed and bound in Spain by GraphyCems

Cover photography © PCL/Alamy

All rights reserved. No part of this publication may be reproduced, stored in a retrieval system or transmitted, in any form or by any means, electronic, mechanical, recording or otherwise, in any part of the world, without prior permission of the publisher. Requests for permission should be made to the publisher at the above address.

Although every care has been taken in compiling this publication, and the contents are believed to be correct at the time of printing, Thomas Cook Tour Operations Limited cannot accept any responsibility for errors or omissions, however caused, or for changes in details given in the guidebook, or for the consequences of any reliance on the information provided. Descriptions and assessments are based on the author's views and experiences when writing and do not necessarily represent those of Thomas Cook Tour Operations Limited.

CONTENTS

INTRODUCING KRAKOW
Introduction 6
When to go 8
Jewish Festival of Culture 12
History 14
Lifestyle 16
Culture 18

MAKING THE MOST OF KRAKOW
Shopping 22
Eating & drinking 25
Entertainment
 & nightlife 29
Sport & relaxation 32
Accommodation 35
The best of Krakow 40
Suggested itineraries 42
Something for nothing 44
When it rains 46
On arrival 48

THE CITY OF KRAKOW
The old town & Wawel 58
Kazimierz 76
Further afield 88

OUT OF TOWN TRIPS
Nowa Huta 102
Zakopane 114

PRACTICAL INFORMATION
Directory 126
Emergencies 136

INDEX 138

MAPS
Krakow 50
Krakow transport map 54
The old town & Wawel 60
Kazimierz 78
Further afield 90
Krakow region 104

POCKET GUIDES

SYMBOLS KEY

The following symbols are used throughout this book:

ⓐ address ⓣ telephone ⓦ website address ⓔ email
🕒 opening times Ⓝ public transport connections ❶ important

The following symbols are used on the maps:

𝑖	information office	▪	point of interest
✈	airport	○	city
✚	hospital	○	large town
⛊	police station	○	small town
🚌	bus station	═	motorway
🚆	railway station	—	main road
†	cathedral	—	minor road
❶	numbers denote featured cafés & restaurants	—	railway

Hotels and restaurants are graded by approximate price as follows:
£ budget price **££** mid-range price **£££** expensive

▶ *The turreted Barbican, gateway to the old town*

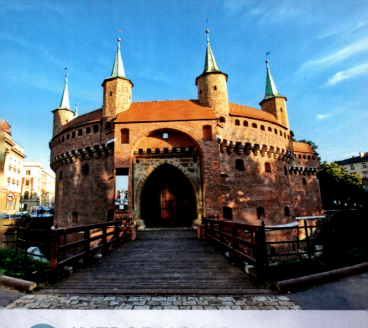

INTRODUCING
Krakow

Introduction

Poland's splendid former capital, Krakow, is the country's number one tourist attraction. A UNESCO-protected old town, extraordinary Jewish heritage and a complicated and often bloody past all add up to make the ancient seat of Polish kings and queens a destination that warrants further investigation. A magnet whose force has drawn in such diverse historical characters as invading Mongol hordes, Lenin and the late Pope John Paul II over the centuries, Krakow offers an irresistible blend of old and new sights and sensations to anyone with the airfare and time to see it.

With just three-quarters of a million inhabitants, Krakow lacks the irritating bustle of the country's delirious capital to the north. An almost provincial feel gives the city a charm that pulls many an unsuspecting tourist into its clutches, making expats out of people who long ago visited for the weekend and who now find themselves married to the girl or boy they met in a bar half a decade ago. But don't let the rustic image fool you. Complete with vast shopping malls and more cutting-edge clubs than you could visit in a month, Krakow is also a modern city, and it's perhaps this heady mix of styles that makes it one of the best destinations in Eastern Europe.

Krakow also enjoys the happy accident of finding itself in the middle of the country's number one tourist region. When you've exhausted the sights and sensations in the city centre, there's still plenty more to discover not too far away. From the unique Socialist Realist sights of nearby Nowa Huta to the numerous attractions on offer in Poland's winter capital, Zakopane, Krakow

INTRODUCTION

is an ideal springboard for prolonged visits that will continue to remain affordable for the next decade at least. With its biscuit-tin architecture, friendly student population and heart-wrenching history, Krakow is a city that demands to be seen.

● *Krakow is a compelling mix of ancient and modern*

INTRODUCING KRAKOW

When to go

SEASONS & CLIMATE
In a country of extremes, 1963 saw winter temperatures in Krakow plummet to −35°C (−31°F), while a few months later people were flopping about in temperatures of +40°C (+104°F). This is the magic of Poland. Whereas Western Europe witnesses year-round temperatures that may barely nudge the mercury, Poland can boast real seasons. With the exception of the usual unexpected downpours, Krakow enjoys hot and sunny summers and the kind of winters that'll keep scarf-makers in business for centuries.

ANNUAL EVENTS
The official events website is at ⓦ www.biurofestiwalowe.pl. The same people publish an excellent bilingual monthly magazine, *Karnet*, full of information about events, concerts and exhibitions throughout the city. Another excellent source of information in English can be found online at ⓦ www.cracow.travel

January
Wieliczka Salt Mines Concert The annual New Year's Concert, 125 m (410 ft) underground in the mind-boggling UNESCO-protected salt mines in Wieliczka. ⓦ www.kopalnia.pl

February
Shanties Landlocked Krakow hosts the annual International Festival of Sailors' Music. ⓦ www.shanties.pl

WHEN TO GO

March
Bach Days Inside one of the city's best-kept secrets, Florianka Hall.
ⓐ Ul Basztowa 8 ⓣ 012 422 51 73

April
Jazz in Krakow A week-long celebration, featuring performers from all over the world. ⓦ www.jazz.krakow.pl

May
Museum Night Cut-price entry to over 20 museums for one night only. Highlights include an after-dark adventure in the Botanic Gardens and the Night of the Hassidim in Kazimierz's Old Synagogue. ⓦ www.mhk.pl

● *Step into spring in Wawel*

Krakow Film Festival The oldest film festival in Poland, showcasing Polish and international shorts and feature-length films of all genres. Ⓦ www.kff.com.pl

June
Great Dragon Parade Outdoor events including concerts, firework displays and flying dragons in the Rynek and other locations. Ⓦ www.paradasmokow.pl
Krakow Opera Summer Starting in June and running for over a month, the city's opera season comes alive with a series of summer concerts. ☎ 012 296 61 00 Ⓦ www.opera.krakow.pl
Lajkonik Parade Always on the first Thursday after Corpus Christi, a rider on a wooden horse dances through town to bring the city good luck for the year. Ⓦ www.mhk.pl
Wianki *Wianki* are candlelit wreaths the young maidens of Krakow send floating down the Wisła River as part of the all-night merrymaking on St John's Day on 24 June. Since the 19th century the ancient pagan festival has been the occasion of a huge fiesta, with fireworks and live music along the river close to Wawel.

July
International Festival of Street Theatre Three days of fire-eating, magic and exotic street performances in the Rynek featuring theatre groups from all over the world. Ⓦ http://teatrkto.pl
Jewish Festival of Culture The big one (see page 12).

August
Pierogi Festival Sample one of the country's favourite national dishes around the city.

September
Dachshund Parade Owners converge in the old town for one glorious day every September to show off their sausage dogs.

October
Organ Days A three-day celebration of an instrument intrinsically linked with Krakow.

December
Christmas Cribs Competition A presentation of the best of the year's famous Christmas cribs in the Rynek. ⓦ www.mhk.pl

---

PUBLIC HOLIDAYS
New Year's Day 1 Jan
Epiphany 6 Jan
Easter Sunday 8 Apr 2012; 31 Mar 2013; 20 Apr 2014
Easter Monday 9 Apr 2012; 1 Apr 2013; 21 Apr 2014
Labour Day 1 May
Constitution Day 3 May
Ascension Day (40 days after Easter) 17 May 2012; 9 May 2013; 29 May 2014
Corpus Christi (Thursday after Trinity Sunday, 60 days after Easter) 7 June 2012; 30 May 2013; 19 June 2014
Assumption 15 Aug
All Saints' Day 1 Nov
Independence Day 11 Nov
Christmas 25 & 26 Dec (Christmas Eve, though not a public holiday, is the traditional day for eating Christmas dinner.)

INTRODUCING KRAKOW

Jewish Festival of Culture

An established fixture on Krakow's annual cultural calendar, the city's huge Jewish Festival of Culture was started in 1988 somewhat controversially by the Roman Catholic Janusz Makuch. Initially a rather bookish event that attempted to bring Polish and Jewish cultures together through intellectual discussion, the festival has ballooned into one of the biggest Jewish cultural events in the world. Attracting visitors and participants from all corners of the globe, the city's traditional Jewish quarter of Kazimierz and the old town are transformed for almost a fortnight into a non-stop celebration of a culture whose followers, up until World War II, made up a quarter of Krakow's population.

As well as a barrage of events for spectators, from poetry recitals to some of the best klezmer music you're ever likely to hear, the festival provides visitors with scores of opportunities to get involved. Helping keep ancient Jewish traditions alive, a range of workshops take place on such diverse subjects as Hasidic dancing, paper cutting, kosher cooking and Hebrew calligraphy. Most of the events are free to attend and many of them are available to English speakers. The festival finishes in spectacular style with a massive free outdoor concert in Kazimierz's ul Szeroka, attracting over 10,000 people who come to listen to music on a huge stage outside the Old Synagogue and sample some fine Jewish food.

Despite cries from some that the festival is nothing more than a clever marketing ploy to exploit Jewish culture and tradition, it continues to grow in size and variety annually. Taking place during Krakow's hottest month, July, the Jewish

JEWISH FESTIVAL OF CULTURE

Festival of Culture is a truly remarkable event that's more than worth attending.

Festival office a Ul Józefa 36 t 012 431 15 17
w www.jewishfestival.pl

Musical performance at the Jewish Festival

INTRODUCING KRAKOW

History

Archaeologists believe the Krakow area was inhabited as far back as 50,000 BC, when a small industrial settlement making primitive tools existed on what's now Wawel Hill. One of the oldest cities in Poland, Krakow was already a thriving Slavic trading city when it was incorporated into the Piast dynasty in around AD 990 and is believed by many to be the birthplace of the modern Polish nation. With the establishment of the bishopric of Krakow in AD 1000 and the construction of Wawel Cathedral soon after, Krakow's fate as an important city was sealed.

In 1038 Krakow became the capital of Poland, a status that lasted until 1596 when the royal court was moved to Warsaw. Although Polish kings and queens continued to be buried in Krakow, the city soon entered a period of decline. During the 18th century Krakow fell victim to a series of sieges and occupations, caught in the middle of the battles for supremacy between Russia, Prussia and Austria. In 1795 Krakow became part of Austria, before a brief period inside Napoleon's Duchy of Warsaw (1807–15) and another interlude as an independent republic (1815–46).

Absorbed back into the Austrian empire in 1846, Krakow became a thriving centre of Polish culture, and the birthplace of the movement for national revival. After independence in 1918 the city became one of the most culturally and politically important cities in the region. On 6 September 1939 the Germans invaded Krakow, wiping out over 700 years of Jewish culture. Poland fell into the communist sphere of influence until 1989. Stalin once famously said that forcing communism on the Poles was like trying to put a saddle on a cow, a statement evidenced by the fact that Poland was the only country behind the Iron Curtain where religious activity was allowed to flourish unhindered.

The construction of the Socialist Realist borough Nowa Huta in the 1950s, an act that was intended to humiliate the religious and conservative population of Krakow, backfired badly, and it was from this district that some of the most outspoken and violent episodes against communist rule came. Krakow's proudest moment arrived in 1978 when its charismatic archbishop, Karol Wojtyła, became Pope John Paul II. With his spiritual and occasional active backing, the threads of communism began to unwind, and by 1989 the country was free again. Now Poland's number one tourist attraction, Krakow has seen enormous changes during recent decades. In 2008 Prime Minister Donald Tusk announced that Poland would adopt the euro in 2011, but the world financial crisis means this has been delayed by several years.

The interior of Wawel Cathedral. Catholicism is central to Polish history

Lifestyle

The cradle of Polish science, art, music and religion, Krakow has a population that is famous for its conservative and religious temperament. The presence of its ancient university has at the same time created a contradictory atmosphere in which open debate, new experiences and a desire to learn about other cultures are equally important. Notoriously careful with their money, Krakow's thrifty inhabitants know

> **KRAKOW & THE POPE**
> Ever since the founding of the first cathedral on Wawel Hill in the 11th century, the citizens of Krakow and the Polish people in general have looked to the Catholic Church for a sense of national unity. Catholicism has been the guiding light through numerous historical calamities, most recently playing a pivotal role in the underground resistance movement against the communist authorities. The late Pope John Paul II, the former Archbishop of Krakow who is now on the fast track to sainthood, is genuinely believed by the Poles to have been a key influence behind the collapse of socialism, and remains an enormous source of pride. His death shocked the nation in ways impossible for an outsider to comprehend. When attempting to untangle the many complexities and inconsistencies of the people of Krakow, it's a good idea to bear this in mind.

LIFESTYLE

◯ *Eating out and socialising are a way of life in Krakow*

how to have a good time without overspending, and, once you get to know them a little better, provide newcomers with a source of deep and affectionate friendship that will last a lifetime. Great lovers of culture, the good people of Krakow are fond of the theatre and consider visiting art galleries, attending live music performances and eating out a national duty. It's thanks to this quality that Krakow can boast one of the liveliest cultural scenes in the country.

With plenty of mountain air in their blood, the locals are deeply attached to nature and take every available opportunity to disappear to the countryside, where many people keep a second home. This is particularly common during August, the traditional month for holidays, when many businesses close their doors and parts of the city resemble a ghost town.

Culture

From Yiddish theatre to sausage dog parades, Krakow is an astonishingly diverse cultural city. Boasting some 30 major theatrical venues, world-class art and Poland's best selection of museums, Krakow offers more culture than many cities twice its size.

Modern Polish theatre began in the 19th century when Krakow was one of the main centres of modernist art in Eastern Europe. Contemporary productions by international playwrights inspired many nationals, including Stanisław Wyspiański (see page 20), who wrote a total of 37 plays, including *Wesele* (*The Wedding*), arguably Poland's greatest, adapted for cinema in 1973 by the Oscar-winning director Andrzej Wajda. Among the city's great theatres are the Groteska Puppet, Mask & Actor Theatre, which stages productions for both children and adults, the Juliusz Słowacki Theatre and the Stary Teatr (Old Theatre), Poland's first.

Krakow has never produced a great composer, although this hasn't stopped it from being a centre of great music for centuries, from klezmer to opera to the diverse repertoire of Nowa Huta's multiple award-winning Steelworks Brass Band. Musical highlights include a visit to the Opera Krakowska, Krakow Filharmonia and Kazimierz's predominantly Jewish-themed Krakow Opera Kameralna.

National icon and Krakow native Jan Matejko (1838–93), Stanisław Wyspiański's teacher, painted bombastic oil paintings depicting historical events, many of which can be seen in the house that bears his name in the old town. As well as the many

CULTURE

historical masterpieces, insight into the 21st-century Polish creative psyche can be found inside galleries throughout Krakow, including the Palace of Art and the small gallery above the Pauza bar (see page 75).

○ *The opulent Juliusz Słowacki Theatre*

INTRODUCING KRAKOW

> **WYSPIAŃSKI**
>
> Architect, painter, playwright and poet, Krakow's creative genius was unquestionably Stanisław Wyspiański (1869–1907). A leading member of the Polish revival *Młoda Polska* (Young Poland) movement, Wyspiański's output was immense. Blending tradition and modernism, he is perhaps best remembered for his imaginative Art Nouveau stained-glass designs that grace several buildings around the city and are mentioned throughout this guidebook. Like all good artistic heroes, Stanisław Wyspiański suffered from both physical and mental illness, and died at the tragically young age of 38. His body lies at rest in the city's Pauline Church (see page 81). The museum opened in his honour (see page 70) is a good place to find out more.

The highlight for most art lovers is the Czartoryski Museum (see page 62), home to Leonardo da Vinci's *Lady with an Ermine*, a rare example of an oil painting by the great man. The diversity and quality of museums in the city will tempt you to make a significant dent in your budget. To get the most out of them, visit during May's extraordinary Museum Night (see page 9) or buy a Krakow Card (see page 44).

▶ *St Mary's Basilica provides a scenic backdrop for Krakow's nightlife*

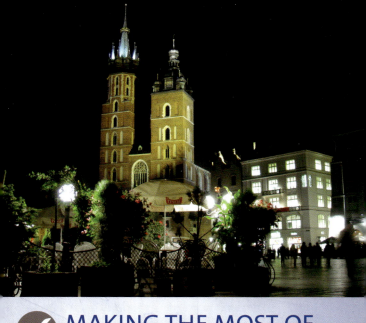

MAKING THE MOST OF
Krakow

MAKING THE MOST OF KRAKOW

Shopping

The first and for some the most important thing to know about shopping in Krakow and Poland in general is that alcohol and cigarettes are cheaper in the street than they are in duty free. Clambering off a 737 clutching a carrier bag full of vodka and Rothmans with a big grin on your face cuts no ice here. Beyond that, the general retail experience is much the same as it is in any other European city. Of course, there are exceptions. Notably, the fabulous Sunday market in Kazimierz (see page 44) and the extraordinary shops selling religious items of every persuasion scattered around the old town. For specific and in-depth coverage of shopping in Krakow, see the relevant 'Retail therapy' sections in this book.

The combination of an emerging middle class and a proliferation of people with disposable incomes has led to a mushrooming of shopping malls all over Krakow. Hardly indicative of traditional Polish culture, malls do at least show the general state of the modern nation, which up until recently had to make do with limited goods of poor quality endorsed by the state. Given the often appalling weather conditions during the winter months, malls, as much as you want to hate them, are a welcome introduction to Krakow's shopping scene.

Galeria Centrum Just off the Rynek, this is the oldest and least ostentatious of the bunch. More of a department store than a mall, really. ⓐ Ul św Anny 2 ⓕ 012 422 98 22 ⓛ 09.30–21.00 Mon–Fri, 10.00–20.00 Sat, 10.00–19.00 Sun

Galeria Kazimierz Complete with a multiplex cinema, this beauty is the only mall in the centre offering entertainment as

SHOPPING ✓

◆ *Icon shopping in the Cloth Hall*

> ### USEFUL SHOPPING PHRASES
>
> **What time do the shops open/close?**
> O której godzinie otwierają/zamykają sklepy?
> *O ktoo-rey go-jee-nyair otvyerayom/za-me-ka-yom skhle-pe?*
>
> **How much is this?** **Can I try this on?**
> Ile to kosztuje? Czy mogę to przymierzyć?
> *Ee-lair toh ko-shtoo-yeh? Che mo-ghair toh pshe-mye-jech?*
>
> **My size is …** **I'll take this one please**
> Mój rozmiar to … Poproszę o to
> *Mooy roz-myarh toh …* *Po-pro-sheh o toh*
>
> **This is too large/too small/too expensive.
> Do you have any others?**
> To jest zbyt duże/zbyt male/zbyt drogie.
> Czy macie coś innego?
> *Toh yest zbit doo-jeh/zbit ma-weh/zbit dro-ghyeh.
> Che ma-che cosh in-ne-go?*

well as shopping. ⓐ Ul Podgórska 34 ⓣ 012 433 01 01 ⓦ www.galeriakazimierz.pl ⓒ 10.00–22.00 Mon–Sat, 10.00–20.00 Sun
Galeria Krakowska A huge beast next to the train station, bursting with glitzy shops and fast-food outlets. ⓐ Ul Pawia 5 ⓣ 012 428 99 00 ⓦ www.galeria-krakowska.pl ⓒ 09.00–22.00 Mon–Sat, 10.00–21.00 Sun

Eating & drinking

People don't come to Krakow for the fine dining. With few exceptions, the Poles still haven't got the hang of cooking anything but their own food, which is thankfully both varied and delicious. Eating in Krakow is a mostly ad hoc affair anyway, an obligatory chore fitted in somewhere between waking up and falling off a barstool. As well as the local food and drink listed below, look out for *pierogi*, a ravioli-type dish served with sour cream instead of tomato sauce and sold in all Polish and many international restaurants. Most staff working in restaurants in the old town speak English and will be able to advise you on what local dishes are on offer.

Picnics are a good summer option, with the Planty (see page 70) and Botanic Gardens (see page 95) offering two excellent places in which to eat under the sky. Despite its profusion of tourists, the centre of Krakow is a heavily populated residential area, with small supermarkets on every street that can provide all the necessary requirements.

As you'll soon notice, there are a lot of small stalls around selling different varieties of bread. The most common is the

> **PRICE CATEGORIES**
> The following price ratings used throughout this guidebook indicate the average price per head for a two- or three-course meal excluding drinks.
> £ up to 30 zł ££ 30–60 zł £££ over 60 zł

precel, a bagel-shaped, plain or seeded white roll, also known as an *obwarzanek*, sold for between 1 zł and 1.50 zł. The other ubiquitous pseudo roll is the *oscypek*. Bearing an uncanny resemblance to a fancy bread roll, *oscypek* is actually a smoked, salty sheep's milk cheese. Originating from the nearby mountains, *oscypki* aren't everyone's cup of tea, but they do provide the perfect accompaniment to the *obwarzanek*, forming the fundamental ingredients for snacking on the hoof or in a park. Sometimes available hot and even offered in miniature versions, a large *oscypek* will set you back around 10 zł.

⬤ *Grab an* oscypek *and you might get a surprise*

EATING & DRINKING

Polish desserts, notably *kremówka* (cream-filled cakes), are worth the plane fare alone. Rumours are that the late Pope John Paul II's final trip to Krakow in 1999 was heavily influenced by the lack of *kremówka* in the Vatican. Sold in many cafés, and in shops by weight, a large piece of *tofinka* (a kind of sweet cake) should be packed in all picnic baskets as standard.

Krakow is reputed to possess the highest concentration of pubs in the world, a strange fact considering that Poland's beer is not generally referred to with awe; Polish vodka on the other hand is up there with the best of the bunch. Brands to watch out for are the aristocratic Chopin and Belvedere, and the more bucolic Żubrówka, which comes with a blade of bison grass in every bottle. The other indigenous tipple of note is *grzaniec Galicyjski*, mulled red wine that's drunk scorching hot. Savouring any alcohol to excess in a public place could result in a sizeable fine or even some unplanned rehab. Polish police are not renowned for their toleration of public inebriation: if you are arrested for being drunk in a public place, you risk being committed to a drying-out clinic from which you will not be released until you are sober, and whose fees you will be responsible for paying.

As Poland becomes more westernised, the propensity to tip is on the increase. Considering the average restaurant employee in Krakow is lucky to take home more than 800 zł (around £170) every month, you may like to help the new trend along. The accepted norm is to give 10 per cent or round up the bill. Finally, one word of warning: saying thank you to your waiter or waitress as you pay is interpreted as an open invitation to pocket the change.

USEFUL DINING PHRASES

I would like a table for ... people
Poproszę o stolik dla ... osób
Po-pro-sheh o sto-leek dla ... o-soob

Waiter/waitress!
Kelner/Kelnerka!
Kelner/Kelnerka!

May I have the bill please?
Poproszę o rachunek?
Po-pro-sheh o ra-hoo-neck?

Could I have it well cooked/medium/rare please?
Poproszę o dobrze/średnio/lekko wysmażone?
Po-pro-sheh o do-bjeh/shre-dnyo/lek-ko ve-sma-jo-ne?

I am a vegetarian. Does this contain meat?
Jetsem wegetarianinem/wegetarianką (fem).
Czy w tym daniu jest mięso?
*Yestem vegetarianinem/vegetariankahng (fem).
Tchee fteem dah-nyoo yest myensoh?*

Excuse me, where is the toilet?
Przepraszam, gdzie jest toaleta?
Pshe-pra-sham, ghjair yest toe-a-lair-tah?

Entertainment & nightlife

Bursting with bearded eccentrics in jazz clubs and scantily clad partygoers in places that sometimes forget to close, Krakow is a hedonist's dream. The distinction between bars and clubs is a little blurred at times, with many places claiming to be a bar hosting all-night sessions where dancing on the tables is considered good form. Many bars advertise their closing time as *do ostatniego klienta* – until the last customer. In short, if you can't find something to do in Krakow after the sun dips behind the gargoyles of the Cloth Hall then you've almost certainly been locked in a church.

The old town is the main place to go clubbing and also boasts the highest concentration of bars, although Kazimierz can claim the more interesting selection of the latter. Table service is the norm in most bars. One word of warning: if you walk past a place that says Night Club, especially outside the city centre, it could well be a brothel.

While in Krakow it would be unforgivable not to sample the city's jazz scene:

Boogie One of the best clubs in town, with a sophisticated feel and some fine performances. ⓐ Ul Szpitalna 9 ⓣ 012 429 43 06 ⓦ www.boogiecafe.pl ⓒ 10.00–02.00 daily

Harris Piano Jazz Bar A smoky underground club with no air conditioning. A classic among jazz clubs. ⓐ Rynek Główny 28 ⓣ 012 421 57 41 ⓦ www.harris.krakow.pl ⓒ 09.00–02.00

U Muniaka A labyrinth of rooms hides the occasional well-known face, including Krakow resident Nigel Kennedy. ⓐ Ul Floriańska 3 ⓣ 012 423 12 05 ⓒ 19.00–02.00 daily

MAKING THE MOST OF KRAKOW

Piec'Art The preserve of the city's better class of jazz hooligan inside a tip-top old-town venue. ⓐ Ul Szewska 12 ⓣ 012 429 64 25 ⓒ 15.00–02.00 daily

Stalowe Magnolie An extraordinary labyrinth of opulence in a pricey and sophisticated venue that puts on quality

○ *A fire dancer lights up the old town*

ENTERTAINMENT & NIGHTLIFE

live music every night. ⓐ Ul św Jana 15 ⓣ 012 422 84 72
ⓦ www.stalowemagnolie.com ⓒ 19.00–02.00 Sun–Thur,
19.00–04.00 Fri & Sat

Krakow is the city in which the failed fireman Krzysztof Kieślowski started his illustrious cinematic career, and where going to the cinema is something the locals like to do a lot. Films are shown in their original language with Polish subtitles. Tickets cost 10–20 zł.

ARS Hollywood blockbusters and the occasional art-house treat in the heart of the city. ⓐ Ul św Jana 6 ⓣ 012 421 41 99

IMAX A monster of a screen. ⓐ Al Pokoju 44 ⓣ 012 290 90 90
ⓝ Tram: 1, 14, 22; Bus: 125

Kino Pod Baranami One of the city's few remaining art-house cinemas and the spiritual home of November's Independent Film Festival. ⓐ Rynek Główny 27 ⓣ 012 423 07 68
ⓦ www.kinopodbaranami.pl

TICKETS

With the exception of major imported acts, ticket prices are low in Poland. Many events in Krakow sell out fast, so buying in advance is highly recommended. For most events such as special club nights, jazz concerts and cinema screenings, tickets should be bought from the venue in question. Theatre and concert tickets can be bought from venues, or from the friendly, English-speaking staff at the **Cultural Information Centre** (ⓐ Ul św Jana 2 ⓣ 012 421 77 87 ⓦ www.karnet.krakow.pl ⓒ 10.00–18.00).

Sport & relaxation

SPECTATOR SPORTS
Football
Two of Poland's oldest and most successful teams play in Krakow, although most people prefer to watch them on television due to the legendary violence on the terraces. Tickets cost buttons and are bought at the ground if you think you're hard enough.
Cracovia ⓐ Kałuży 1 ⓣ 012 427 35 62 ⓦ www.cracovia.pl
ⓝ Tram: 15, 18; Bus: 109, 134, 409
Wisła ⓐ Reymonta 22 ⓣ 012 630 76 00 ⓦ www.wisla.krakow.pl
ⓝ Tram: 15, 18

PARTICIPATION SPORTS
Cycling
Bike One Krakow has 16 stands of bicycles available around the city in spring and summer. Would-be riders must first register online and pay a subscription of 15 zł for seven days; the first 30 minutes' rental is free, the next half-hour is 1.50 zł and subsequent hours are 2 zł each. ⓐ Pl Wszystkich Świętych, Wawel, Miodowa, Pl Wolnica, and at least a dozen other city locations ⓣ 012 358 96 42 ⓦ www.bikeone.pl ⓛ Apr–mid-Nov

Extreme sports
Reni Sport Climbing walls, the real thing (including professional training) in the Tatra Mountains, plus other nutty things to do including the inevitable bungee jumping. ⓐ Ul Czepca 11
ⓣ 012 638 07 34 ⓦ http://renisport.pl ⓝ Tram: 4, 8, 13

SPORT & RELAXATION

◐ Cyclists take a rest in front of the Jagiellonian University Museum

MAKING THE MOST OF KRAKOW

Golf
Krakow Valley Golf & Country Club An 18-hole course 40 km (25 miles) west of Krakow, plus driving range, hotel, conference centre and horse-riding facilities. A one-way taxi trip costs about 400 zł. ⓐ Paczółtowice 328, Krzeszowice ⓣ 012 258 60 00 ⓦ www.krakow-valley.com

Swimming
Park Wodny The undisputed king of swimming pools, with water slides, health and beauty facilities and a decent café. ⓐ Ul Dobrego Pasterza 126 ⓣ 012 616 31 90 ⓦ www.parkwodny.pl ⓛ 08.00–22.00 ⓝ Bus: 125, 128, 129, 132, 138, 139, 142, 152, 169, 182, 425

Winter sports
If you don't want to travel to Zakopane (see page 114), the city's indoor ice-skating rinks are a good choice:
Lodowisko Krakowianka Home to the local professional ice-hockey team; skate rental available. ⓐ Ul Siedleckiego 7 ⓣ 012 421 13 17 ⓦ www.cracovia.pl ⓛ 60-min sessions, times vary daily (Sept–Apr) ⓝ Tram: 1, 7, 9, 11, 14, 22; Bus: 128, 184
Lodowisko w Krakowie ⓐ Ul Eisenberga 2 ⓣ 012 418 41 56 ⓦ www.lodowisko-krakow.pl ⓛ Opening times vary daily (Nov–Mar) ⓝ Tram: 4, 9, 10, 15, 32, 40; Bus: 124, 125, 128, 152, 184, 188, 424, 425

Accommodation

Even though prices creep up every year, the cost of hotel accommodation in Krakow remains laughable in comparison to the West. This not only makes the city an attractive budget option, but also means visitors can afford to base themselves in a more central location. However, the old town can be rowdy at night, and consequently not much fun, particularly for those travelling with children. Likewise, hostels can be noisy affairs. If you're looking for a good night's sleep in the centre, choose something just a little further out.

HOSTELS
Good Bye Lenin £ A standard hostel experience. The communist theme is fun but really little more than a cheap marketing gimmick. ➋ Ul Joselewicza 23 (Further afield) ➊ 012 421 20 30 ⓦ www.goodbyelenin.pl

> **PRICE CATEGORIES**
> The following price ratings, used throughout this guidebook, indicate the average price per double room, including breakfast, per night. The prices listed are subject to change depending on whether you book during the high or low season. In Zakopane, the high season includes the period roughly between Christmas and the end of February.
> **£** up to 150 zł **££** 150–300 zł **£££** over 300 zł

MAKING THE MOST OF KRAKOW

Mama's £ With a distinctly feminine feel, Mama's keeps things basic meaning a great location can be affordable for all.
ⓐ Ul Bracka 4 (The old town & Wawel) ⓣ 012 429 59 40
ⓦ www.mamashostel.com.pl

Seventh Heaven £ Bright colours and tatty furniture are the order of the day here. Very popular with English-speaking backpackers and budget travellers. ⓐ Ul Lenartowicza 7 (Further afield) ⓣ 012 633 38 87 ⓦ www.seventhheaven.pl

Lemon Hostel £–££ A ten-minute walk from the old town, Lemon Hostel offers a pleasant environment with rooms named after fruit. ⓐ Ul Straszewskiego 25 (The old town & Wawel)
ⓣ 012 633 51 48 ⓦ www.lemonhostel.pl

Hostel Rynek 7 ££ One of the best addresses in Krakow. Relaxed, with the larger dormitories offering spectacular views of the Rynek.
ⓐ Rynek Główny 7/6 (The old town & Wawel) ⓣ 012 431 16 98
ⓦ www.hostelrynek7.pl

Nathan's Villa ££ This little venture offers good service and infamous all-night parties in the basement. ⓐ Ul św Agnieszki 1 (Further afield) ⓣ 012 422 35 45 ⓦ www.nathansvilla.com

APARTMENTS

2nd Floor ££ Plastic furniture and pink pillowcases for the discerning gay budget traveller. A recommended introduction into the still very much nascent world of gay Krakow. Note that there's no breakfast provided here, but a small kitchen is available

ACCOMMODATION

○ *Several hostels, such as Hostel Rynek 7, offer superb views of the market square*

free of charge for guests. Also note that it really only caters to gay guests. ⓐ Ul Królewska 84 (Further afield) ⓣ 012 602 320 206 ⓦ http://2ndfloor.queer.pl

Affinity Flats ££–£££ Heaps of stylish and well-renovated apartments throughout the city, from modest accommodation in grey blocks to the ultimate luxury pad in the old town. ⓐ Ul Brzozowa 17 (Kazimierz office; locations throughout the city) ⓣ 012 421 05 68 ⓦ www.affinityflats.com

Red Brick Apartments £££ Offering a great location just west of the train station and north of the old town, this classy establishment provides 16 magnificent apartments, including kitchens and Wi-Fi Internet. A touch pricey, but worth every penny. ⓐ Ul Kurniki 3 (Further afield) ⓣ 012 628 66 00 ⓦ www.redbrick.pl

HOTELS

Hotel Saski ££ A fabulous option for those looking for a relatively cheap sleep in the old town, Saski offers rococo splashes, an antique lift and a bit of money left in your pocket to explore the choice of quality restaurants along the street it's located on. ⓐ Ul Sławkowska 3 (The old town & Wawel) ⓣ 012 421 42 22 ⓦ www.hotelsaski.com.pl

Hotel Pollera ££–£££ Close to the train and bus stations, Pollera's classy Art Nouveau chic comes with a price, but the combination of location, impeccable service and the fabulous Wyspiański stained-glass window on the staircase makes this

ACCOMMODATION

one a tempting offer for travellers looking to push the boat out a bit while taking in the sights and sensations of the city.
ⓐ Szpitalna 30 (The old town & Wawel) ⓣ 012 422 10 44
ⓦ www.pollera.com.pl

RT Monopol £££ A nicely renovated hotel immediately east of the old town, with views over the Planty. It's popular with tour groups and features all manner of extras including good facilities for disabled travellers, its own car park for visitors and the option of bringing your pet with you if you can't bear to be parted. ⓐ Ul św Gertrudy 6 (The old town & Wawel) ⓣ 012 422 76 66 ⓦ www.rthotels.com.pl

Stary £££ A perfect blend of medieval elegance and modern charm, if you're in Krakow on business at somebody else's expense or you've just won the lottery you couldn't do much better than this place. The perfect 5-star experience, including a swimming pool in the cellar and a great rooftop bar with superb views of the old town. ⓐ Ul Szczepańska 5 (The old town & Wawel) ⓣ 012 384 08 08 ⓦ http://stary.hotel.com.pl

Wielopole £££ A choice of excellent-value singles, doubles and triples a couple of minutes east of the old town. The rooms are basic but clean, the buffet breakfast in the basement is better than many, and the staff seem to be under the distinct impression that you're paying five times the price you really are for your room. ⓐ Ul Wielopole 3 (Further afield) ⓣ 012 422 14 75
ⓦ www.wielopole.pl

THE BEST OF KRAKOW

Whether you're planning a flying visit or staying longer to savour the city, there's more than enough to hold your interest in Krakow. The following sights, places and experiences should not be missed.

TOP 10 ATTRACTIONS

- **Wawel** The spiritual home of the Polish nation, this breathtaking ensemble of buildings justifies Krakow's reputation as one of the most beautiful cities in Europe (see page 67).

- **St Mary's Basilica** The richly decorated interior of St Mary's mirrors perfectly the deeply religious essence of Poland and its people (see page 64).

- **Hejnał** This bugle call is sounded live every hour from the top of St Mary's tallest spire – and has been since 1241 (see page 66).

- **Cloth Hall** Arguably the best-located tourist market in Europe, this medieval shopping mall has always been at the heart of city life (see page 59).

- **Remuh Cemetery** The city's oldest surviving Jewish cemetery is a poignant place in which to start unravelling the tale of an ancient culture that was almost wiped out in the flicker of an eye (see page 80).

- **Da Vinci** A trip to the extraordinary Czartoryski Museum offers visitors a rare glimpse of one of the world's few Leonardo da Vinci masterpieces (see page 62).

- **Lazy afternoons in the Planty** Pack a Polish picnic and head for the shade of the fabulously green and peaceful city-centre park (see page 70).

- **Traditional Polish food** Take a fairy-tale adventure into traditional local cuisine as provided by one of the branches of the unforgettable U Babci Maliny (see page 72).

- **Discovering Wyspiański** Explore Krakow's abundance of Art Nouveau stained-glass masterpieces, bequeathed to the city by the late Stanisław Wyspiański (see page 20).

- **Kazimierz's bric-a-brac** Rifle through the flea markets and antique shops of Kazimierz and be inspired by its quirkily decorated bars and cafés (see page 44).

Krakow's ancient and scenic city skyline

MAKING THE MOST OF KRAKOW

Suggested itineraries

HALF-DAY: KRAKOW IN A HURRY
Head for the Rynek, pick up a daft souvenir in the Cloth Hall, then spend a few minutes contemplating the masterpieces inside St Mary's Basilica. If you need refreshment, enjoy one of the square's cafés and watch the world go by before taking a wander around the rest of the area, popping into a museum if time allows.

1 DAY: TIME TO SEE A LITTLE MORE
As well as the above recommendations, take time to explore the majesty of Wawel Cathedral before heading south for a tour of the old Jewish area of Kazimierz. Don't miss the Remuh Synagogue and its cemetery, and be sure to take some time to visit the poignant exhibitions at the nearby Galicia Jewish Museum. If you've got more time, spend 30 minutes or more inside the amazing Ethnographical Museum before finishing the evening in a traditional Jewish restaurant followed by a beer or two in one of Kazimierz's wacky bars.

2–3 DAYS: TIME TO SEE MUCH MORE
Add to the above itinerary the full Wawel experience, itself a day's work if you do it properly, and spend any remaining time making the most of Krakow's museums. Explore the sights of the Jewish ghetto in Podgórze and get out to Nowa Huta if you can, to see its impressive Socialist Realist architecture. Use your evenings to sample the best of the city's restaurants, bars and clubs.

SUGGESTED ITINERARIES

LONGER: ENJOYING KRAKOW TO THE FULL
Precisely what this guidebook's been written for. Get the most out of the best Krakow has to offer, including a leisurely adventure in Nowa Huta and a night or two in Zakopane.

◐ *Under the arches, Krakow central market square*

MAKING THE MOST OF KRAKOW

Something for nothing

A few days in Krakow are hardly going to make a large dent in your wallet, but it's still nice to be able to enjoy the city without having to pay for the pleasure. The most obvious way of getting something for nothing is to explore Krakow's many churches. With the exception of St Mary's Basilica, all the churches in the old town are free to enter. Remember that men should remove their hats when entering a Catholic church (the reverse for a synagogue) and keep their legs and, if possible, arms covered. Women are expected to cover their shoulders. Most museums open their doors for free one day a week, which, if you pack a few in, can save you a fair amount of cash.

The higgledy-piggledy jumble of buildings in Kazimierz offers a wealth of opportunities to browse an amazing array of junk, old communist-era consumer goods, antiques, fur coats and much more in an ever-increasing number of shops. The extraordinary old Jewish market offers a different experience

KRAKOW CARD
Available in both two-day (50 zł) and three-day (65 zł) versions, the Krakow Card gives users free access to more than 30 museums plus unlimited travel on the city's public transport system. Like other similar cards, it also offers discounts in shops and restaurants. Available at many hotels and tourist information centres.
ⓦ www.krakowcard.com

SOMETHING FOR NOTHING

every day, from clothes to cabbages to a brilliant, large **Sunday market** (@ Pl Nowy ⏲ Best times to visit 10.00–12.00; opens earlier in summer), which features the best selection of bric-a-brac to be found in the city.

If you've already bought one of the recommended books listed on page 135, you could do a lot worse than to take advantage of the city walks included in them. Covering some of the more obscure sights in the old town, Kazimierz and Nowa Huta, these really well-thought-out tours can add a whole new dimension to the city.

◯ *Kazimierz's Sunday market – a browser's paradise*

MAKING THE MOST OF KRAKOW

When it rains

There are a million things to do if it rains in Krakow, from delving deep underground in Wawel Cathedral's extraordinary crypts and the Dragon's Cave to just sitting and watching the world go by in a café. Perhaps the best way to use up a few wet hours is to take advantage of some of the lesser-known museums in the city.

Among the countless exhibits at the **Archaeology Museum** (Ul Poselska 3 012 422 71 00) are some particularly interesting models of life in Małopolska as it was lived during the Stone Age, an exceptional collection of reproductions of the type of clothing worn in the region from 70,000 BC until the founding of the old town, and a mysterious 9th-century pagan stone totem pole, found nearby.

Nathan of Nathan's Villa fame (see page 36) has taken his hobby into the public realm and opened a large aquarium inside the glorious surroundings of the city's former Natural History Museum, naming it **Krakow Aquarium** (Ul św Sebastiana 9 012 429 10 49 www.aquariumkrakow.com). Although some of the old museum's exhibits are still on display upstairs, including a preserved Ice Age woolly rhinoceros, most of the building has been taken over by tanks full of live sharks, exotic reptiles and other eerie beasts. Aimed at children but of interest to all, many of the exhibits come with computer-aided presentations and there's also the option of special guided tours. Even if reptiles aren't exactly up your street, the magnificent Art Nouveau surroundings are worth a look in themselves.

WHEN IT RAINS

Located inside a wonderful 15th-century building, Krakow's brilliant **Pharmacy Museum** (Ul Floriańska 25, 012 421 92 79, www.muzeumfarmacji.pl) includes all manner of exhibits from full-scale reproductions of ancient apothecary shops to some beastly snakes in jars and, on the top floor, a really good display of traditional herbal medicines. Also of interest is the small exhibit dedicated to the extraordinary and brave Pole Tadeusz Pankiewicz (see the Museum of National Remembrance, page 94).

Escape the rain at the Pharmacy Museum

MAKING THE MOST OF KRAKOW

On arrival

TIME DIFFERENCE
Poland's clocks are on Central European Time (CET, or GMT+1). During Daylight Saving Time (late Mar–Oct), the clocks are put forward by one hour.

ARRIVING
By air
All flights to Krakow arrive at **Balice Airport** (ⓦ www.krakow airport.pl), which is also known as John Paul II International Airport, 18 km (11 miles) west of the city. You'll find tourist information, public telephones, ATMs, 24-hour currency exchange and kiosks selling snacks and SIM cards in the airport's combined international arrivals and departures hall. A small terminal immediately northeast of the international terminal deals with all internal flights.

The quickest way into town is by taxi, of which those marked **Radio Taxis** (❶ 012 191 91) outside the main exit are the cheapest and most reliable (30–50 zł into town). The most economical way of getting into the centre of Krakow is by train. A free shuttle bus outside the international terminal building takes you to the airport's train station. You can buy your ticket (10 zł) on board the train, which travels non-stop to Krakow's main train station, Dworzec Główny. The journey time is 18 minutes, and trains run around the clock, every 30 minutes during the day and less frequently at other times. Buses from outside the terminal are even cheaper than the trains, but these take a long time to get into town.

ON ARRIVAL

By rail
Krakow's main train station (Dworzec Główny) remains the least convivial of all options listed here. Find currency exchange (🕐 06.00–22.00) and ATMs, plus scores of kiosks selling snacks and SIM cards. The hostel touts who work the train station are almost certainly going to rip you off. Ignore them. Walk through the underpass into the Planty and follow the path into the old town, or take a taxi if you're travelling further afield.

By road
All international buses arrive at the modern central bus station on ul Bosacka (🌐 www.rda.krakow.pl). Facilities are basic, but there are clean toilets, an ATM and a surprisingly good buffet restaurant (🕐 07.15–21.45). The old town is a few hundred metres to the southwest and can be reached by the underpass that goes under the platforms of the central train station next door. Alternatively, taxis are parked outside night and day.

FINDING YOUR FEET
The general pace of life in Krakow is blissfully slow, which, with the exception of when you want something to eat, couldn't be much better. It's safer than most Western European cities too. Beware of the grinning 20-somethings, complete with leather jackets and dogs, who like to prowl ul Floriańska and the Planty looking for beer money. They're harmless but irritating.

ORIENTATION
Most of Krakow's sights and hotels are on the northern shore of the Wisła River, which runs through the city. The old town,

MAKING THE MOST OF KRAKOW

ON ARRIVAL

MAKING THE MOST OF KRAKOW

Wawel and Kazimierz are all next to each other in a line running more or less north to south, and can be walked to and from without any problem. The city centre is small enough for you never to worry about getting lost but if you do find yourself up a gum tree just ask a local. They don't bite.

GETTING AROUND

Unless you have difficulty walking over relatively short distances or are in Krakow for just a few hours, everything there is to see within the old town and Kazimierz can be seen on foot. For trips further afield, the city's tram service is second to none, and taxis remain a ludicrously cheap way of covering long distances.

Trams

Fast, cheap, efficient, and with the added bonus of being able to slip through the city's increasingly snarling traffic without

◐ *Get out and about – take a tram*

ON ARRIVAL

> **IF YOU GET LOST, TRY ...**
>
> **Excuse me, do you speak English?**
> Przepraszam, czy mówi pan/pani po angielsku?
> *Pshe-pra-sham, che moo-vee pan/pa-nee poe an-gyels-koo?*
>
> **Excuse me, is this the right way to the old town/the city centre/the tourist office/the train station/the bus station?**
> Przepraszam, czy dojdę tędy do starego miasta/centrum miasta/biura turystycznego/dworzec kolejowy/dworca autobusowego?
> *Pshe-pra-sham, che doy-dair ten-di doe sta-re-go mya-stah/sten-troom mya-stah/byoo-rah too-ri-sti-chne-go/dvo-zhets ko-le-yo-vi/dvortsah awto-boo-so-vego?*
>
> **Can you point to it on my map?**
> Czy móglby pan/moglaby pani pokazać to na mapie?
> *Che moog-wbe pan/mog-wa-be pa-nee poka-zach na ma-pyair?*

hindrance, trams run 05.00–23.00 (w www.mpk.krakow.pl). A single-journey ticket (also valid on buses) costs about 3 zł. Better value are 24-hour (approx 11 zł), 48-hour (approx 19 zł) and 72-hour (25 zł) tickets, which can be bought from kiosks near stops or anywhere you see a *sprzedaż biletów MPK* sign. Validate your ticket in the machine on board and away you go.

MAKING THE MOST OF KRAKOW

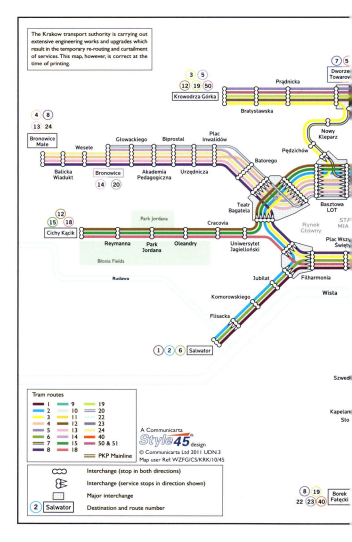

ON ARRIVAL

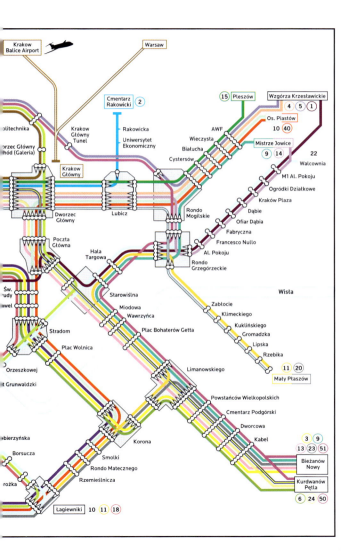

MAKING THE MOST OF KRAKOW

Taxis
Taxis are cheap and form a vital part of the city's after-dark make-up. The standard charge for a taxi ride is around 7 zł, with a further 2.50 zł or so per kilometre (²/₃ mile) after that and a higher rate of 3.50 zł at night. If a taxi has a large sign on the roof with the name and telephone number of the company, you can rest assured that, as long as you make sure the driver switches the meter on before you depart, you won't be ripped off.
Barbakan ❶ 196 61/800 400 400 (free number)
MPT Radio Taxi ❶ 196 63/012 644 55 55/800 444 444 (free number)
Radio Taxi Wawel ❶ 196 66/012 266 66 66/800 66 66 66 (free number)

CAR HIRE
Hiring a car is a waste of money unless you're planning excursions outside the city. Parking is difficult and tightly controlled in the city too. Shopping around secures the best deal, as many discounts are available; prices vary up to about 450 zł a day. All the big car-hire companies have offices at the airport which keep longer hours.
Avis ⓐ Ul Lubicz 23 ❶ 0601 20 07 02 ⓦ www.avis.pl
Budget ⓐ Ul Balicka 4 ❶ 012 637 00 89 ⓦ www.budget.com.pl
Europcar ⓐ Ul Szlak 2 ❶ 012 633 77 73 ⓦ www.europcar.com

❶ Car crime is rife, so use one of the city's guarded parking areas or choose a hotel with secure parking facilities

▶ *Wawel's royal castle towers above Krakow*

THE CITY OF
Krakow

THE CITY

The old town & Wawel

Saved the indignity of being turned to rubble at the end of World War II like Poland's other great cities, Krakow's Stare Miasto (old town) is quite simply flabbergasting. A UNESCO-protected site since 1978, the old town was founded in 1257 and still retains most of its original features. Wawel, just south of the old town, is essentially the birthplace of the nation. Both areas deserve plenty of attention.

SIGHTS & ATTRACTIONS

Archdiocesan Museum
Next door to here was once the home of a young, sports-mad Polish priest called Karol Wojtyła who went on to become Pope John Paul II. This museum holds a reconstruction of his rooms as well as changing exhibitions of religious and sacred artefacts. ⓐ Ul Kanonicza 19–21 ⓣ 012 421 89 63 ⓦ www.muzeumkra.diecezja.pl ⓞ 10.00–16.00 Tues–Fri, 10.00–15.00 Sat & Sun ⓘ Admission charge

Barbican
Built in 1498, the Arabesque-inspired Barbican looks like something out of a fairy tale. The seven-turreted structure features fearsome walls that are 3 m (10 ft) thick, pierced with 130 arrow loops. Along with the Floriańska Gate just to the south, the Barbican is by far the best-preserved example of the city's original defences. ⓐ Ul Basztowa ⓣ 012 422 98 77 ⓦ www.mhk.pl ⓞ 10.30–18.00 May–Oct ⓘ Admission charge

THE OLD TOWN & WAWEL

Burgher Museum (Hippolit House)

This charming museum features room upon room of re-creations of bourgeois living conditions in the city from the 17th to the 20th century. ⓐ Pl Mariacki 3 ⓣ 012 422 42 19 ⓦ www.mhk.pl ⓛ 10.00–17.30 Wed–Sun (May–Oct); 09.00–16.00 Wed & Fri–Sun, 12.00–19.00 Thur (Nov–Apr); closed on 2nd Sun of the month ⓘ Admission charge; free on Wed

Cloth Hall

The imposing Cloth Hall, or Sukiennice, started life as two walls between which local traders would store their goods at night. Its present appearance owes most to the visionary Renaissance labour of the 16th-century Italian architect Giovanni il Mosca and a few neo-Gothic additions in the 19th century. The Cloth

● *The massive Barbican*

THE CITY

THE OLD TOWN & WAWEL

THE CITY

Hall was where the local medieval elite came to buy the latest designer fabrics, but its most famous patron was none other than Lenin, who was a frequent visitor to the Noworolski café (see page 73) between 1912 and 1914. On the ground floor stalls sell a well-priced range of souvenirs, from swords to amber necklaces to leather handbags. On the first floor the paintings in the Gallery of 19th-Century Polish Art show the highlights of the age. ⓐ Rynek Główny 1–3 ⓣ 012 424 46 00 ⓦ www.muzeum.krakow.pl ⓒ Gallery open 10.00–20.00 Tues–Sat, 10.00–18.00 Sun. Terraces and café open 10.00–23.00 daily ⓘ Admission charge for gallery

Czartoryski Museum
The main building of this world-class collection is closed for renovation until about 2013. During this time the museum's star masterpieces, the Leonardo Da Vinci oil painting, *Lady with an Ermine*, and Rembrandt's *Landscape with the Good Samaritan*, may travel on loan to various galleries abroad. At the time of going to press, the museum was also in talks to arrange for them to be exhibited in between these other showings at the Bishop Erazm Ciołek Palace in ul Kanonicza. Meanwhile, the Czartoryski's Ancient Art Gallery, with splendid examples of works from Greece, Etruria, Egypt and Rome, has reopened in the nearby Arsenal building. ⓐ Ul Pijarska 8 ⓣ 012 422 55 66 ⓦ www.muzeum.krakow.pl ⓒ 10.00–16.00 Tues–Sun ⓘ Admission charge

Historical Museum of Krakow
Traditionally the venue for the annual exhibition of Christmas cribs made by local adults and children, the Historical Museum

THE OLD TOWN & WAWEL

of Krakow at the Krzysztofory Palace is under renovation until at least 2014, when a new exhibition of the city's history is to be mounted here. Some temporary exhibitions are planned so it is worth putting your nose through the door. ⓐ Rynek Główny 35 ⓣ 012 619 23 00 ⓦ www.mhk.pl ⓛ Opening times vary ⓘ Admission charge

Jagiellonian University Museum

Founded by King Kazimierz in 1364, the Jagiellonian University ranks as the third-oldest university in Europe. The museum contains many glorious pieces including the oldest surviving globe to show the Americas. ⓐ Ul Jagiellońska 15 ⓣ 012 663 15 21, 012 663 13 07 ⓦ www.maius.uj.edu.pl ⓛ 10.00–15.00 Mon, Wed & Fri, 10.00–14.00 Sat (year-round); also open 10.00–18.00 Tues & Thur (Apr–Oct); 10.00–16.00 Tues, 10.00–15.00 Thur (Nov–Mar). Last tour 40 mins before closing time ⓘ Admission charge. Guided tours only. Booking recommended.

Rynek Główny

Krakow's undisputed focal point is its main market square Rynek Główny, or just plain Rynek. Laid out in 1257, the 200-m x 200-m (656-ft x 656-ft) square was once the largest medieval square in Europe. Originally the centre of life in the city, the Rynek was formerly a frenetic bustle of commercial activity, where Jews, Germans, Poles and others sold their wares. Krakow's post-communist reinvention of itself has ensured that the Rynek is once again the city's favourite place to see and be seen in.

THE CITY

Rynek Underground

This recently opened excavation 4 m (13 ft) under the market square traces its history back to the Celts and beyond. As well as artefacts from the archaeological excavations which reveal 800 years of uninterrupted trade on this site, there is a multimedia exhibition showing Krakow's place at the heart of European life.
ⓐ Rynek Główny 1 ❶ 012 426 50 04 ⓦ www.mhk.pl ❶ 10.00–20.00 Wed–Mon, 10.00–16.00 Tues. Last entry 60 mins before closing time ❶ Admission charge; free on Mon

St Francis's Basilica

First consecrated in 1269, St Francis's is notable as being the first brick building in the city. The current neo-Gothic structure houses some of the finest Art Nouveau stained glass in Europe, produced by Stanisław Wyspiański (see page 20) between 1895 and 1904. ⓐ Pl Wszystkich Świętych, off Franciszkańska ❶ 012 422 53 76 ⓦ www.franciszkanska.pl ❶ 09.45–16.15 Mon–Sat, 13.15–16.15 Sun (closed during Mass and prayers)

St Mary's Basilica

The basilica owes its present Gothic appearance to building work carried out in the middle of the 14th century; venture inside and you'll be picking your jaw up off the floor. Ablaze with colour and breathtaking sculptures, its centrepiece is the 15th-century altar by the German artist Veit Stoss (Wit Stwosz, c. 1447–1533). Stoss's painted limewood carving depicts the Virgin Mary among the Apostles, and is the largest Gothic altar in Europe. Legend has it the church's two unequal towers were built by two competitive brothers, each trying to outdo the

THE OLD TOWN & WAWEL

○ *The magnificently decorated interior of St Mary's Basilica*

THE CITY

other. From the top of the taller, left-hand one a fireman plays the Hejnał, an hourly bugle call that has sounded round the clock since 1241, when, it's said, a sentry gave warning of a Tatar invasion. ⓐ Pl Mariacki 5 ⓣ 012 422 05 21 ⓦ www.mariacki.com ⓞ Church open 11.30–18.00 Mon–Sat, 14.00–18.00 Sun (altar opens at 11.50). Tower open 09.00–11.30 & 13.00–17.30 Tues, Thur & Sat (May–Aug) ⓘ Admission charge for both

SS Peter & Paul's Church

Having almost fallen down as construction was nearing completion at the start of the 17th century, the Baroque SS Peter & Paul's Church (Kościól św Piotra i Pawła) has been

> **WAWEL DRAGON**
>
> Smok Wawelski was a particularly offensive dragon who allegedly lived in a cave under Wawel Hill and whose hobbies included terrorising local sheep and the occasional virgin. He gobbled up many handsome young heroes, until a humble local cobbler tricked the dragon into eating a sheep that had been stuffed with tar and sulphur. The result was explosive: the dragon was vanquished forever, the hero won the king's daughter, inherited the kingdom and they all lived happily ever after. Even the dragon had an afterlife – as a statue breathing real fire on the banks of the river. His cave is open to the public. ⓐ Cave entrance on top of western side of Wawel Hill ⓣ 012 422 51 55 ⓦ www.wawel.krakow.pl ⓞ 10.00–17.00 daily (Apr–June, Sept & Oct); 10.00–20.00 daily (July & Aug) ⓘ Admission charge; free for under-7s

THE OLD TOWN & WAWEL

dicing with disaster ever since. The city's main Jesuit church suffered a minor indignity during the short-lived days of the Republic of Krakow when it was handed over to the Greek Orthodox Church. Inside find a feast of delights including the remains of the 17th-century priest Piotr Skarga buried in the crypt. ⓐ Ul Grodzka 54 ⓘ 012 350 63 65 ⓒ 08.00–20.00 daily

Wawel Hill & Royal Castle
The national symbol of patriotism, strength and unity for both secular and religious Poles, the breathtaking ensemble of buildings perched on top of the 25-m (82-ft)-high Wawel Hill rates as a must-see attraction for anyone with even a passing interest in history. Construction of the first cathedral began soon after the founding of the bishopric of Krakow in AD 1000, with numerous additions made over the passing centuries. It was the main residence of Polish royalty from the 11th to the 17th century and the final resting place of numerous Polish kings, queens and national heroes. Highlights include the cathedral, the state rooms of the Royal Castle and the armoury collection. Tickets for the Cathedral Museum (see below) and the different parts of the castle are sold separately although it is possible to buy discounted combined tickets. It's a good idea to book in advance in summer as there is a daily limit on the number of visitors. The ticket office closes 1 hour 15 minutes before the exhibitions. ⓘ 012 422 51 55 ext 219 ⓔ informacja@wawel.edu.pl

Cathedral Museum The exhibits include some of Poland's most prized religious and royal treasures from the 13th century onwards. Tickets include admission to the tower of the giant

Zygmunt bell and the Royal Tombs. ❶ 012 429 33 21
Ⓦ www.katedra-wawelska.pl 🕒 09.00–17.00 Mon–Sat
(Apr–Sept); 09.00–16.00 Mon–Sat (Oct–Mar) ❶ Admission
charge for museum; free entry to cathedral

Lost Wawel This underground museum displays the finds
uncovered during archaeological excavations on Wawel Hill,
including parts of the first church, the Rotunda of the Virgin
Mary, dating from around the 10th century. ❶ 012 422 51 55
Ⓦ www.wawel.krakow.pl 🕒 09.30–13.00 Mon, 09.30–17.00
Tues–Fri, 11.00–18.00 Sat & Sun (Apr–Oct); 09.30–16.00
Tues–Sat, 10.00–16.00 Sun (Nov–Mar) ❶ Admission charge, free
on Mon (Apr–Oct); free on Sun (Nov–Mar)

Oriental Art A rich hoard of carpets, tapestries, weapons and
arms from Turkey, the Crimea, the Caucasus and Persia. Exhibits
include King Jan III Sobieski's haul of treasure, tents and
banners. 🕒 09.30–17.00 Tues–Fri, 10.00–17.00 Sat & Sun
(Apr–Oct); 09.30–16.00 Tues–Sat (Nov–Mar) ❶ Admission
charge. Advance reservation essential Nov–Mar

State Rooms and Royal Apartments These floors offer intriguing
insights into life at the Polish royal court. Of particular note are
the extensive collection of Brussels tapestries commissioned by
Zygmunt August and the Envoys' Room, whose 16th-century
ceiling once featured 194 carved heads of the king's subjects.
The 30 that remain are mysteriously compelling. ❶ 012 422 51 55
Ⓦ www.wawel.krakow.pl 🕒 State Rooms open 09.30–17.00
Tues–Fri, 11.00–18.00 Sat & Sun (Apr–Oct); 09.30–16.00

THE OLD TOWN & WAWEL

Tues–Fri, 09.30–16.00 Sat, 10.00–16.00 Sun (Nov–Mar). Royal Apartments open same times as State Rooms but closed Sun (Nov–Mar) ● Admission charge for both; State Rooms free on Sun (Nov–Mar)

● Wawel's spectacular cathedral

THE CITY

> **PLANTY PICNIC**
> Dating from the mid-19th century, when the old city walls were knocked down, the magnificent 21-hectare (52-acre) park known as the Planty surrounds almost the entire old town. Take advantage of the city's army of street vendors, kebab stalls and markets, make yourself up a picnic and bring it here for an interesting and alternative lunch option.

Treasury & Armoury Memorabilia of the Polish monarchs are set inside fabulous 15th-century Gothic chambers. Among the many fine examples is the *Szczerbiec*, the original coronation sword. ● 09.30–13.00 Mon, 09.30–17.00 Tues–Fri, 11.00–18.00 Sat & Sun (Apr–Oct); 09.30–16.00 Tues–Sat (Nov–Mar) ● Admission charge; free on Mon (Apr–Oct)

Wawel Cathedral Wawel's spectacular cathedral has been called the most important building in Poland. Inside the 14th-century walls you will find elaborate chapels, tombs, huge bells and great works of art. ● 012 429 95 15/6 ● www.katedra-wawelska.pl ● 09.00–17.00 Mon–Sat, 12.30–17.00 Sun (Apr–Sept); 09.00–16.00 Mon–Sat, 12.30–16.00 Sun (Oct–Mar) ● Admission charge to cathedral museum; cathedral itself free

Wyspiański Museum
Exhibits include Wyspiański-related temporary shows as well as permanent displays such as his original stained-glass designs

THE OLD TOWN & WAWEL

and a rather extraordinary model of Wawel. ⓐ Ul Szczepańska 11 ⓣ 012 422 70 21 ⓦ www.muzeum.krakow.pl ⓛ 10.00–18.00 Tues–Sat, 10.00–16.00 Sun ⓘ Admission charge

CULTURE

Juliusz Słowacki Theatre

Built on the site of a medieval church demolished to make way for it, the Paris Opéra-inspired theatre's construction caused an uproar among Krakow's conservative elite when it was opened in 1893. ⓐ Pl św Ducha 1 ⓣ 012 424 45 28 ⓦ www.slowacki.krakow.pl ⓛ Opening times vary according to performance

RETAIL THERAPY

A fool and his money are easily parted, especially in the old town. Nevertheless, it is where you will find the best range of souvenirs, arts and crafts and fashion boutiques.

Galeria Ora Here you'll find high-quality modern jewellery in silver, amber and unusual gemstones created by contemporary Polish designers, mainly working in and around Krakow. ⓐ Ul św Anny 3/1a ⓣ 012 426 89 20 ⓦ www.galeria-ora.com ⓛ 10.00–20.00 Mon–Sat, 11.00–18.00 Sun (Apr–Nov); 10.00–18.00 Mon–Sat, 10.30–16.00 Sun (Dec–Mar)

Wawel Established in 1898, Wawel makes its own range of chocolates, including many in fancy tins and packages that make superb gifts. ⓐ Rynek Główny 33 ⓣ 012 423 12 47 ⓦ www.wawel.com.pl ⓛ 10.00–19.00 daily

TAKING A BREAK

U Babci Maliny £ ❶ One of the best places to devour plates of home-cooked *pierogi* in Krakow. Unmissable. ⓐ Ul Sławkowska 17 ⓣ 012 422 76 01 ⓦ www.kuchniaubabcimaliny.pl ⓛ 11.00–21.00 Mon–Fri, 12.00–21.00 Sat & Sun. Another branch at ⓐ Ul Szpitalna 38 ⓣ 012 421 48 18 ⓛ 11.00–23.00 daily

Café Camelot £ ❷ Simple light meals, salads and apple cake, with 13th-century stone walls and bags of ambience. ⓐ Ul św Tomasza 17 ⓣ 012 421 01 25 ⓛ 09.00–24.00 daily

Chimera Salad Bar £ ❸ A few doors away from its more upmarket parent restaurant this cheery self-service place is a Krakow landmark. ⓐ Ul św Anny 3 ⓣ 012 292 12 12 ⓦ www.chimera.com.pl ⓛ 09.00–22.00 daily

Tram Bar £ ❹ Old wooden tram seating and tram paraphernalia, good coffee and riotous Saturday-night karaoke sessions. ⓐ Ul Stolarska 11 ⓣ 012 423 22 55 ⓛ 07.30–24.00 Mon–Fri, 11.00–24.00 Sat & Sun

U Zalipianek £ ❺ Crochet tablecloths and traditional floral designs on the walls in one of the city's most beloved communist-era leftovers. ⓐ Ul Szewska 24 ⓣ 012 422 29 50 ⓛ 09.00–22.00 daily

THE OLD TOWN & WAWEL

Noworolski ££ ❼ Gorgeous Art Nouveau rooms that once saw Lenin scribbling letters home to his mum, Noworolski offers coffee and cakes served by well-behaved waiters dressed as penguins. ⓐ Rynek Główny 1 (Cloth Hall) ⓣ 012 422 47 71 ⓦ www.noworolski.com.pl ⓒ 09.00–24.00 daily

AFTER DARK

RESTAURANTS

Zapiecek Polskie Pierogarnie £ ❼ Tiny and oh so quaint, on a good day you'll catch them making the deliciously large and ridiculously cheap *pierogi* served on plastic plates.
ⓐ Ul Sławkowska 32 ⓣ 012 422 74 95 ⓒ 24 hrs

Aqua e Vino ££ ❽ Italian run and owned, the menu includes a wide range of good-looking Italian dishes, plus there's a superb wine list to complement. ⓐ Ul Wiślna 5/10 ⓣ 012 421 25 67 ⓦ www.aquaevino.pl ⓒ 12.00–22.45 daily

Metropolitan ££ ❾ Chess sets, supermodel waitresses and the delightful smell of bacon... Metropolitan is by far the best place in or out of the old town for enjoying a hearty breakfast at any time of day. ⓐ Ul Sławkowska 3 ⓣ 012 421 98 03 ⓦ www.metropolitan-krakow.com ⓒ 07.30–23.00 Mon–Sat, 07.30–15.00 Sun

Miód Malina ££ ❿ A good range of local and Italian dishes served to a clientele including loyal locals and tourists alike. Their large upmarket Polish restaurant **Wesele** (ⓐ Rynek

Główny 10) is also highly recommended. ⓐ Ul Grodzka 40
❶ 012 430 04 11 🕐 12.00–23.00 daily

Paese ££ ⓫ Quality Corsican cuisine on two floors; try the
excellent fondue. ⓐ Ul Poselska 24 ❶ 012 421 62 73 Ⓦ www.
paese.com.pl 🕐 13.00–23.00 daily

Cyrano de Bergerac £££ ⓬ White tablecloths and gorgeous
tapestries in a charming cellar; the French menu reads like a poem.
ⓐ Ul Sławkowska 26 ❶ 012 411 72 88 Ⓦ www.cyranode
bergerac.pl 🕐 12.00–24.00 Mon–Sat

Wierzynek £££ ⓭ A Polish-international restaurant that has
entertained everyone from Fidel Castro to Steven Spielberg
since it first opened its doors in 1364. ⓐ Rynek Główny 15
❶ 012 424 96 00 Ⓦ www.wierzynek.com.pl 🕐 13.00–23.00 daily

▲ *Wierzynek has been offering fine dining for centuries*

THE OLD TOWN & WAWEL

BARS & CLUBS

Boom Bar Rush An ear-blistering collection of corridors and a busy dance floor. ⓐ Ul Gołębia 6 ⓣ 012 429 39 74 ⓦ www.boombarrush.com ⓞ 20.00–last customer daily

Cień Endless waves of house music in a rather informal brick cellar atmosphere. ⓐ Ul św Jana 15 ⓣ 012 422 21 77 ⓞ 21.00–04.00 Tues & Wed, 21.00–05.00 Thur, 21.00–06.00 Fri & Sat

Irish Mbassy A vast pub on three floors offering everything from Playstation events to pub quizzes to curry nights. Lads' heaven. ⓐ Ul Stolarska 3 ⓦ www.irishmbassy.com ⓞ 12.00–01.00 Mon–Thur, 12.00–last customer Fri, 10.00–last customer Sat & Sun

Jazz Rock Café There's nothing new or sophisticated about this basement joint in the heart of the old town. Kids fall in every night and never leave. ⓐ Ul Sławkowska 12 ⓣ 0508 89 00 26 ⓦ www.jazzrockcafe.pl ⓞ 16.00–04.00 daily

U Louisa This place is something of an expat magnet thanks to the deadly combination of gorgeous barmaids and cold German lager. ⓐ Rynek Główny 13 ⓣ 012 617 02 22 ⓦ www.ulouisa.com ⓞ 11.00–last customer daily

Pauza This hidden gem is the preserve of a bunch of arty drinkers who play good music and run a small gallery upstairs showcasing young contemporary artists. ⓐ Ul Floriańska 18/3 ⓞ 10.00–24.00 Mon–Sat, 12.00–24.00 Sun

THE CITY

Kazimierz

The perfect antidote to the antiquated excesses of the old town, Kazimierz was established as a settlement in the 14th century to break the monopoly of the German merchants in neighbouring Krakow. The spiritual home of the city's once large Jewish community, Kazimierz's post-communist reputation as an undesirable location full of arty types was all but obliterated when Steven Spielberg chose it as one of the main locations for shooting *Schindler's List* in 1992. Now a thriving Jewish-heritage tourist destination as well as the location of some of the best bars and cafés in Krakow, Kazimierz offers a beguiling mix of sights and sensations with a distinctively edgy feel that many visitors find impossible to resist.

SIGHTS & ATTRACTIONS

JEWISH KAZIMIERZ
Galicia Jewish Museum
Housed inside an old Jewish factory, this superb museum organises a range of photographic exhibitions and also has a good café and bookshop. ⓐ Ul Dajwór 18 ⓘ 012 421 68 42 ⓦ www.galiciajewishmuseum.org ⓛ 10.00–18.00 daily ⓘ Admission charge

Isaac's Synagogue
Dating from 1644, this Judaic-Baroque synagogue is still in the process of renovation. The stunning interior is a must-see. Also of interest are the old black-and-white films on show, depicting

KAZIMIERZ

Jewish life in Kazimierz before World War II. ⓐ Ul Kupa 18
ⓣ 012 430 55 77 ⓒ 09.00–19.00 Sun–Fri ⓘ Admission charge

Old Synagogue

The oldest preserved synagogue in Poland, believed to date from the early 15th century, and now a fine museum and bookshop.
ⓐ Ul Szeroka 24 ⓣ 012 422 09 62 ⓦ www.mhk.pl ⓒ 10.00–14.00 Mon, 09.00–17.00 Tues–Sun (Apr–Oct); 10.00–14.00 Mon, 09.00–16.00 Wed, Thur, Sat & Sun, 10.00–17.00 Fri (Nov–Mar)
ⓘ Admission charge; free on Mon

▲ *The Old Synagogue, Kazimierz*

THE CITY

KAZIMIERZ

THE CITY

Remuh Synagogue & Cemetery

Built in 1553 and renovated in 1829, the spectacularly restored Remuh Synagogue is the only remaining active Orthodox synagogue in Krakow. Of Kazimierz's three remaining Jewish cemeteries, the one here is by far the most interesting. In use until 1800, it contains the graves of many of Krakow's most important religious and secular Jews. Perhaps the most famous of all the graves, many of which are in the old Jewish style before it became fashionable for Jews to model their graves along Christian design, is that of the 16th-century Rabbi Moses

◐ *The Remuh Cemetery – final resting place of many of Krakow's Jews*

Isserles, better known as the Remuh, who was the son of the synagogue's founder. ⓐ Ul Szeroka 40 ⓣ 012 429 57 35 ⓦ http://krakow.jewish.org.pl ⓞ 09.00–18.00 Sun–Fri (May–Oct); 09.00–16.00 Sun–Fri (Nov–Apr). Closed during services and for 2 hrs before Fri services ⓘ Admission charge

OTHER SIGHTS & ATTRACTIONS
City Engineering Museum
Two museums in one, this place offers a brilliant collection of old cars, trams and other forms of motorised transport, as well as the rather bizarre Fun & Science exhibition. ⓐ Ul św Wawrzyńca 15 ⓣ 012 421 12 42 ⓞ 10.00–16.00 Tues–Sun ⓘ Admission charge

Ethnographical Museum
Situated inside Kazimierz's former town hall in what was once the centre of its grand market square, this often overlooked museum offers a fascinating insight into local Polish folk culture. ⓐ Pl Wolnica 1 ⓣ 012 430 55 75 ⓦ www.etnomuzeum.eu ⓞ 11.00–19.00 Tues, Wed, Fri & Sat, 11.00–21.00 Thur, 11.00–15.00 Sun ⓘ Admission charge

Pauline Church
Way back in 1079 the Bishop of Krakow, Stanisław Szczepański, found himself on the wrong end of an accusation of treason from King Bolesław the Bold. The bishop was subsequently beheaded, and as so often happens in the stuff of legend the royal family fell under a curse. To appease Szczepański's spirit the family built this fine church, which, as well as having one

> **PLAC NOWY**
> With the exception of the rather charming red-brick rotunda at its centre dating from 1900, Plac Nowy, Kazimierz's central marketplace and modern spiritual focal point, is something of a blot on the landscape. However, as a snapshot that defines what Kazimierz was and is, there's nothing better. A microcosm of local history, Plac Nowy was until the outbreak of World War II the city's Jewish market, with the rotunda serving as the ritual slaughterhouse. Now the area has grown into something of an anomaly, with a fine daily market (see page 44), kebab stalls frequented by the local folk, and a ring of bars and cafés overflowing with Krakow's moneyed bohemian 20-somethings.

of the best stories in Krakow behind its existence, is also the final resting place of Stanisław Wyspiański. ⓐ Ul Skałeczna 15 ⓘ 012 421 72 44 ⓒ 09.00–17.00 daily ⓘ Admission charge

CULTURE

Jewish Cultural Centre

Opened in 1993 under the auspices of the Judaica Foundation, the Jewish Cultural Centre operates out of a beautifully renovated 19th-century prayer house and offers educational programmes, lectures and other Jewish-related services to the whole community. The centre also organises the annual

KAZIMIERZ

Bajit Chadasz (Jewish Cultural Month) every autumn. ⓐ Ul Meiselsa 17 ❶ 012 430 64 49 ⓦ www.judaica.pl ❶ Times vary according to events

RETAIL THERAPY

For information on the fabulous bric-a-brac shops and market in Kazimierz, see page 44.

High Fidelity A true labour of love courtesy of one of Kazimierz's distinctly different characters. Find among the wall-to-wall collection of rare vinyl several oddball releases from the 70s and 80s as well as the occasional communist-issue Western classic.
ⓐ Ul Podbrzezie 6 ❶ 0506 18 44 79 ⓔ lysyania@interia.pl
❶ 12.00–16.00 Mon–Fri, 11.00–14.00 Sat

TAKING A BREAK

Bagelmama £ ❶ The best bagels in Poland, and it's a fine place to visit for its relaxed atmosphere and good food including a selection of above-average Mexican dishes. ⓐ Ul Dajwór 10
❶ 012 346 16 46 ⓦ www.bagelmama.com ❶ 09.00–20.00 Mon–Sat, 09.00–19.00 Sun

Les Couleurs £ ❷ Hot croissants and an existential-looking rabble in this French-inspired gap filler. Reminiscent of a classic Parisian bar, down to the reams of smoke and jocular bar staff.
ⓐ Ul Estery 10 ❶ 012 429 42 70 ❶ 07.00–02.00 Mon–Fri, 08.00–02.00 or until last customer Sat & Sun

THE CITY

Kolanko No 6 £ ❸ If you can find a better spot anywhere on the planet run by a plumber, named after a piece of plumbing pipe and containing a dentist's chair, then you certainly get about. Good music, average coffee and fine pancakes. ⓐ Ul Józefa 17 ⓣ 012 292 03 20 ⓦ www.kolanko.net ⓛ 12.00–last customer Mon–Fri, 11.00–last customer Sat & Sun

Singer £ ❹ Refusing to fit any category at all, Singer is one of those bars that helps a newcomer feel at home and fall in love with Krakow. The unique atmosphere – bizarre sewing-machine theme and all – will have you returning again and again. ⓐ Ul Estery 20 ⓣ 012 292 06 22 ⓛ 09.00–last customer daily

AFTER DARK

RESTAURANTS
Mleczarnia £ ❺ Like drinking on the set of *Steptoe and Son* with the cast of *The Rocky Horror Picture Show*, this classic Kazimierz haunt offers a great place for an afternoon pick-me-up or more lively adventures after the sun goes down. ⓐ Ul Rabina Beera Meiselsa 20 ⓣ 012 421 85 32 ⓛ 10.00–last customer daily

Bombaj Tandoori ££ ❻ A seemingly hastily converted Polish cafeteria. The ambience is provided by throwing a few ethnic prints on the walls, splashing out on a Best of Bollywood CD and keeping the lights down low. The Indian food stands head and shoulders above most spicy options available countrywide. ⓐ Ul Szeroka 7 ⓣ 012 422 37 97 ⓦ www.restauracjabombaj.pl ⓛ 12.00–23.00 Sun–Thur, 12.00–24.00 Fri & Sat

KAZIMIERZ

Edo ££ ❼ Exquisitely prepared sushi and other Japanese favourites inside something that wouldn't look out of place in a Kyoto backstreet. It's excellent value too. Put on some clean socks before booking a table in the private area. ⓐ Ul Bożego Ciała 3 ⓣ 012 422 24 24 ⓦ www.edosushi.pl ⓛ 12.00–22.00 Sun–Thur, 12.00–23.00 Fri & Sat

Klezmer Hois ££ ❽ Located inside the old Jewish bathhouse, this veritable jumble sale of a restaurant offers fine traditional dining at its best. Even the hordes of tourists fail to rub you up the wrong way, it's that good. Live Jewish music every evening adds to the magic. ⓐ Ul Szeroka 6 ⓣ 012 411 12 45 ⓦ www.klezmer.pl ⓛ 08.00–23.00 daily

◐ *Underneath the arches at Pepe Rosso*

THE CITY

Pepe Rosso ££ ❷ A bit of an anomaly for Kazimierz, there are neither gimmicks nor weirdos to be found here, just a highly recommended menu of Italian dishes served professionally inside either a lovely old vaulted cellar or a bright minimalist setting on the ground floor. ⓐ Ul Kupa 15 ⓣ 012 431 08 75 ⓦ www.peperosso.pl ⓒ 12.00–23.00 daily

BARS & CLUBS

Alchemia The best thing in Krakow or a pretentious pit depending on where you stand, Alchemia is the city's unofficial headquarters of hip. Features include a self-service bar, theatre and live music performances. ⓐ Ul Estery 5 ⓣ 012 421 22 00 ⓦ www.alchemia.com.pl ⓒ 09.00–02.00 Mon–Thur, 09.00–04.00 Fri & Sat, 09.00–03.00 Sun

Club Clu Choose from chic conversations on large white sofas to space-age adventures on a dance floor that plays a mixed variety of good music. ⓐ Ul Szeroka 10 ⓣ 012 429 26 09 ⓒ 18.00–last customer daily

Mechanoff Green and metallic, spooky and very Polish, what is in itself a bar of note most nights of the week transforms itself on Wednesdays and Saturdays into a venue for some of the city's more outspoken and eccentric DJs. ⓐ Ul Estery 8 ⓣ 012 422 70 98 ⓒ 18.00–last customer daily

Moment A large metallic bar, glassed-in beer garden and masses of clocks on the walls create a memorable backdrop for the great and the good of Kazimierz to descend nightly for intense

KAZIMIERZ

sessions of booze and chatter. ⓐ Ul Józefa 34 ⓣ 0668 03 40 00 ⓦ www.momentcafe.pl ⓛ 09.00–01.00 daily

Opium Completely refurbished but still darkly red and overflowing with beautiful young professionals. Best of all here is the terrace. ⓐ Ul Jakuba 19, off Ul Józefa ⓣ 012 421 94 61 ⓔ opium@opium.krakow.pl ⓛ 16.00–last customer Mon–Sat, 10.00–01.00 Sun

Propaganda A recommended wander behind the former Iron Curtain and one of the best communist-themed bars in the old communist bloc, this dark and moody drinking hole is littered with miscellaneous bygones from old radios to Lenin posters to some of the people who drink here. Expect a mixed crowd and a late night. ⓐ Ul Miodowa 20 ⓣ 600 33 19 22 ⓛ 12.00–05.00 daily

Pub Stajnia Tour guides point this out since the archway into the bar's courtyard was used in the film *Schindler's List*, but once through that arch you'll find a pleasant green seating area for summer. Year-round, the air-conditioned bar and restaurant are a place to party for those who like 80s and Latin music – with positively no hip-hop or techno. ⓐ Ul Józefa 12 ⓣ 012 423 72 02 ⓦ www.pubstajnia.pl ⓛ 11.00–24.00 daily

Le Scandale A vast array of backlit bottles marks this one out as a place where the young, beautiful and rich come to identify with the Kazimierz buzz. ⓐ Pl Nowy 9 ⓣ 012 430 68 55 ⓛ 07.00–last customer daily

THE CITY

Further afield

Adding to the magic on offer in the city centre are a handful of other treats. Grab a 24-hour public transport ticket (see page 53) and whisk yourself away to one or two of Krakow's more distant tip-top attractions.

△ *Monument commemorating the medieval battle of Grunwald*

FURTHER AFIELD

SIGHTS & ATTRACTIONS

NORTH
Celestat
The oddest museum in a quirky city, Celestat celebrates the Bractwo Kurkowe (Brotherhood of Fowlers). From medieval times this guild (whose most famous son was Marcin Oracewicz) was charged with training local citizens – the butchers, bakers and dumpling-makers – to guard the city against the frequent Tatar attacks. Now more a symbolic

> **GRUNWALD MONUMENT**
> Celebrating the joint Polish-Lithuanian victory over the Teutonic Knights at the Battle of Grunwald on 15 July 1410, sculptor Antoni Wiwulski's (1877–1919) monument was unveiled in front of 160,000 people on the 500th anniversary of the battle in 1910. The original monument was destroyed by the occupying Nazis during World War II and wasn't rebuilt until 1976. Taking pride of place on his horse is the Polish King Władysław Jagiełło. At the front is his cousin Witold, a Lithuanian prince, and at either side are the Polish and Lithuanian armies. At the foot of the monument lies a dead Urlich von Jungingen, the so-called Grand Master of the Teutonic Order, whose dithering policy over Poland saw his demise at the battle.
> Pl Matejki Tram: 2, 3, 4, 7, 12, 13, 14, 15, 20, 24; Bus: 124, 152, 424

THE CITY

FURTHER AFIELD

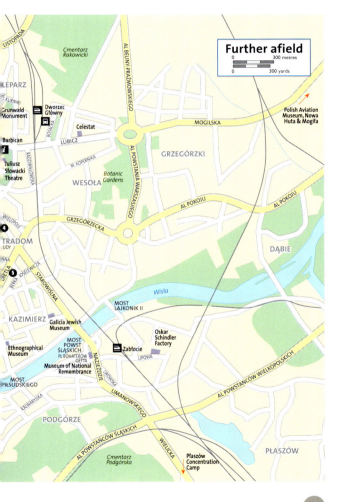

THE CITY

organisation, the brothers still dress in lavish regalia on special city occasions and elect an annual king. 🅐 Ul Lubicz 16 🅣 012 429 37 91 🅦 www.mhk.pl 🅞 Open for special exhibitions only; times vary

SOUTH
Fabryka Oskara Schindlera (Oskar Schindler Factory)
Anyone who has seen the Steven Spielberg film *Schindler's List* knows the story of Oskar Schindler, told in this exhibition of Krakow under Nazi occupation, which opened in his former factory in 2010. Born into a wealthy family in the Moravian town of Zwittau in 1908, Schindler joined the Nazi party not long before the Germans invaded Poland in 1939. He soon moved to Krakow and took over this enamel factory. Above all he was a businessman, supplying the German war effort with goods made by Jewish prisoners from the Podgórze ghetto. However, as the situation worsened Schindler was able to evacuate many of his workers to Moravia, saving them from execution or death in the concentration camps. 🅐 Ul Lipowa 4 🅣 012 257 10 17 🅦 www.mhk.pl 🅞 10.00–16.00 Mon, 10.00–20.00 Tues–Sun (Apr–Oct); 10.00–14.00 Mon, 10.00–18.00 Tues–Sun (Nov–Mar); closed on 1st Mon of the month 🅣 Tram: 7, 9, 11, 13, 24, 50, 51; Bus: 127, 158 🅘 Admission charge; free on Mon

Manggha Centre
A cultural centre championing all things Japanese, this fabulous modern building draws the eye from Wawel Hill and elsewhere. As well as special exhibitions, exhibits include Japanese artefacts such as woodcuts, porcelain, samurai armour and

FURTHER AFIELD

hilarious contemporary Japanese comics. The café is good too.
⊙ Ul Konopnickiej 26 ⊙ 012 267 27 03 ⊙ www.manggha.
krakow.pl ⊙ 10.00–20.00 Tues–Sun (Apr–Sept); 10.00–18.00
daily (Oct–Mar) ⊙ Tram: 1, 2, 6, 18, 19, 22; Bus: 100, 103, 109, 112,
114, 124, 128, 162, 164, 173, 179, 184, 194, 439, 444
⊙ Admission charge

● *Bust of Marcin Oracewicz outside the Celestat*

THE CITY

Museum of National Remembrance
The former site of the Apteka Pod Orłem (Pharmacy Under the Eagle), run by Tadeusz Pankiewicz, the only Gentile allowed to live inside the Podgórze ghetto, is now a poignant museum portraying ghetto life with the aid of a series of moving and disturbing films and photographs. ❸ Pl Bohaterów Getta 18 ❶ 012 656 56 25 ❿ www.mhk.pl ❻ 10.00–14.00 Mon, 09.30–17.00 Tues–Sun (Apr–Oct); 10.00–14.00 Mon, 09.00–16.00 Tues–Thur, 10.00–17.00 Fri (Nov–Mar); closed

PŁASZÓW CONCENTRATION CAMP
Built on the site of two Jewish cemeteries in 1942, initially as a work camp for Polish, German and Jewish workers, the large and now overgrown camp at Płaszów just east of Podgórze rose to infamy soon after the arrival of the sadistic camp commandant Amon Goeth at the start of 1943, when 6,300 Krakow ghetto inhabitants were moved here. The scene of massive and brutal torture against Jews, Roma and others, there's little left to see now, except for a few monuments scattered around. To get there take tram 9, 13, 32 or 34 a couple of stops south from Plac Bohaterów Getta to the Cmentarz Podgórski stop, walk up the hill and take the first right on to ul Jerozolimska. Follow the road until you reach the second camp sign and take the path to the right. The main memorials are on top of the hill to the left, just past the cave. Remember that you're walking on a mass grave site.

FURTHER AFIELD

on 1st Tues of the month ⓝ Tram: 7, 9, 11, 13, 24, 50, 51; Bus: 127, 158 ⓘ Admission charge; free on Mon

Podgórze

The fate of Krakow's sleepy southern suburb of Podgórze changed forever between 3 and 21 March 1941 when the entire Jewish population of the city was moved into a tiny part of the district that became the Jewish ghetto. Cut off from the rest of the city by a 3-m (10-ft)-high wall, some 16,000 Krakow Jews were crammed into just 320 houses and subsequently worked to death or taken to similar or worse fates at the nearby Płaszów concentration camp or the gas chambers of Auschwitz-Birkenau, 80 km (50 miles) to the west. On 13 and 14 March 1943, almost two years to the day after the Nazis created it, the ghetto in Podgórze was finally liquidated. Many traces of it can still be found. There are two remaining sections of the original ghetto wall on the right-hand side of ul Lwowska as you're heading south from pl Bohaterów Getta, and another larger section at ul Limanowskiego 13 a little further on.

EAST
Botanic Gardens

Founded in 1783, Poland's oldest botanic gardens offer 10 hectares (25 acres) of verdant diversions in the city. ⓐ Ul M Kopernika 27 ⓣ 012 663 36 35 ⓦ www.ogrod.uj.edu.pl ⓒ Gardens open 09.00–19.00 (Apr–mid-Sept); 09.00–17.00 (mid-Sept–Mar). Glasshouses close 60 mins before gardens and are closed Fri. Botanic museum open 10.00–14.00 Wed & Fri, 11.00–15.00 Sat

Tram: 4, 5, 9, 10, 14, 15, 20, 40, 51; Bus: 115, 124, 125, 128, 152, 182, 184, 185, 192, 287, 292, 424, 425 ● Admission charge

Polish Aviation Museum
Flying machines here range from early wooden boneshakers to a large field of mostly Soviet-era fighter jets. The hangar behind the ticket office contains a perfectly preserved Spitfire. ● Al Jana Pawła II 39 ● 012 640 99 60 ● www.muzeumlotnictwa.pl ● 09.00–16.00 Tues–Fri, 10.00–16.00 Sat & Sun (Tues outdoor exhibition only open) ● Tram: 1, 4, 5, 9, 10, 14, 15, 22, 40; Bus: 121, 163, 174 ● Admission charge

WEST
History of Photography Museum
The only museum in the country given over entirely to photography is small and scruffy, but if photography is your thing then do yourself a favour and go and have a look. Among the temporary exhibitions are several small rooms packed with old photographic equipment and some exceptional old black-and-white prints of the city. ● Ul Józefitów 16 ● 012 634 59 32 ● www.mhf.krakow.pl ● 11.00–18.00 Wed–Fri, 10.00–15.30 Sat & Sun ● Tram: 4, 8, 13, 14, 20, 24 ● Admission charge

Kościuszko Mound
If you haven't had enough exercise clambering up and down from the city's cellar bars, try climbing this very Polish monument, one of four such man-made mounds around Krakow of varying antiquity and legend. A couple of miles from the city centre, the Kopiec Kościuszki was raised in the 1820s to

FURTHER AFIELD

commemorate Poland's national hero, the military leader Tadeusz Kościuszko. On a fine day you will get a good view of the landscape and be able to find out more about the man and the tradition of making mounds from a small museum in the old fortifications. ⓐ Al Waszyngtona 1 ⓣ 012 425 11 16 ⓦ www.kopieckosciuszki.pl ⓒ Mound open 09.00–dusk Mon–Thur, 09.00–23.00 Fri–Sun (May–Sept); 09.00–dusk daily (Oct–Apr). Exhibition open 09.00–16.30 daily ⓝ Bus: 700 ⓘ Admission charge

Krakow Zoo

As zoos go in Eastern Europe, this one is better than many. It has the added benefit of being in the middle of the fine green space that is Las Wolski. ⓐ Ul Kasy Oszczędności Miasta Krakowa 14 ⓣ 012 425 35 52 ⓦ www.zoo-krakow.pl ⓒ 09.00–14.00 daily ⓝ Bus: 134 from the stop outside Hotel Cracovia (opposite the National Museum of Art) ⓘ Admission charge

● *The Kościuszko Mound – an impressive tribute to a national hero*

THE CITY

National Museum of Art
One of the best museums in Poland. On the top floor there's a dazzling array of Polish art from the Young Poland art movement. ⓐ Al 3 Maja 1 ⓣ 012 295 56 00 ⓦ www.muzeum.krakow.pl ⓛ 10.00–18.00 Tues–Sat, 10.00–16.00 Sun ⓝ Tram: 15, 18; Bus: 103, 114, 144, 152, 164, 169, 173, 179, 192, 194 ⓘ Admission charge; free permanent exhibitions on Sun

TAKING A BREAK

Coffeeheaven £ ❶ The best coffee in the city with quality sandwiches. ⓐ Ul Karmelicka 8 ⓣ 012 421 30 85 ⓛ 07.00–21.30 Mon–Fri, 08.00–21.30 Sat, 09.00–21.00 Sun ⓝ Tram: 4, 8, 14, 15

Massolit Books & Café £ ❷ A combined bookshop and café. Drop by for coffee, good books, carrot cake, and all sorts of entertainment from poetry to music. ⓐ Ul Felicjanek 4 ⓣ 012 432 41 50 ⓦ http://massolit.com ⓛ 10.00–20.00 Sun–Thur, 10.00–21.00 Fri & Sat ⓝ Tram: 1, 2, 3, 6

Rózowy Słoń £ ❸ Pink-and-green furniture, massive comic strips on the walls, a good-value salad bar, *pierogi* and pancakes. ⓐ Ul Straszewskiego 24 ⓣ 012 422 10 00 ⓛ 10.00–20.00 Mon–Sat, 11.00–19.00 Sun ⓝ Tram: 1, 2, 36; Bus: 103, 502

Vega ££ ❹ Feminine and terribly cutesy, this is the best place around to demolish plates of good vegetarian food and huge salads. ⓐ Ul św Gertrudy 7 ⓣ 012 422 34 94 ⓦ http://vegarestauracja.com.pl ⓛ 09.00–21.00 daily ⓝ Tram: 8, 10, 18, 36, 38, 40

AFTER DARK

RESTAURANTS

San Sebastian ££ ❸ A good choice for nouvelle cuisine and dangerously potent cocktails. If you just need a quick snack, try their sublime pâté and toast. ⓐ Ul św Sebastiana 25 ⓣ 012 429 24 76 ⓛ 10.00–24.00 daily ⓝ Tram: 19, 22; Bus: 128, 184, 603, 609

U Ziyada ££ ❾ A beguiling mix of Polish and Kurdish cooking inside a charming castle with breathtaking views of the Wisła. The setting and affordable food on offer more than make up for the long journey necessary to get here. ⓐ Ul Jodłowa 13 ⓣ 012 429 71 05 ⓦ www.uziyada.krakow.pl ⓛ 10.00–21.00 daily ⓝ Bus: 409

BARS & CLUBS

Café Szafé The 'café in a wardrobe' is a cosy bolt-hole where you are almost certain to make friends. There's live music at the weekends, an art gallery and film screenings on Tuesdays. ⓐ Ul Felicjanek 10 ⓣ 0663 90 56 52 ⓦ www.cafeszafe.com ⓛ 09.00–last customer Mon–Fri, 10.00–last customer Sat & Sun ⓝ Tram: 1, 2, 3, 6

Kitsch Tuesday is girls' night, but boys get cheap beer on Wednesdays at this gay-friendly place promising 'freak and crazy parties' until morning comes. ⓐ Ul Wielopole 15/2 ⓣ 012 422 52 99, 0508 40 41 53 ⓦ www.kitsch.pl ⓛ 19.00–05.00 Sun–Wed, 19.00–07.00 Thur–Sat ⓝ Tram: 1, 7, 9, 10, 11, 22; Bus: 609, 614

THE CITY

Łubu Dubu A 70s-style set of rooms in which to dance, drink and occasionally sit in a puddle of beer and watch a cult movie on the big screen. ⓐ Ul Wielopole 15/2 ⓣ 0694 46 14 02 ⓦ www.lubu-dubu.pl ⓛ 18.00–03.00 Sun–Tues, 18.00–04.00 Wed, 18.00–05.00 Thur, 18.00–06.00 Fri & Sat

Panorama Mediocre international food courtesy of indifferent waitresses, only worth mentioning for the spectacular view of the city from the terrace. A good spot for a summer beer, however. Find it above the Jubilat shopping centre, through an unmarked door on the right. Enter the lift and push button number 1. ⓐ Ul Zwierzyniecka 50 ⓣ 012 422 28 14 ⓦ www.panoramaklub.eu ⓛ 11.00–22.00 ⓝ Tram: 1, 2, 6; Bus: 109, 409

Qube Inside the Sheraton Hotel, so the bar bill in this fine vodka joint will probably hurt more than the hangover. Over 200 vodkas and a splendid atrium setting. ⓐ Ul Powiśle 7 ⓣ 012 662 16 74 ⓦ www.sheraton.pl/krakow ⓛ 08.00–24.00 daily ⓝ Tram: 1, 2, 6; Bus: 109, 409

Someplace Else Gorgeous barmaids and overpriced drinks in the Sheraton's sports bar. A good place to watch football and meet some of the city's more interesting expats. ⓐ Ul Powiśle 7 ⓣ 012 662 10 00 ⓦ http://krakow.someplace-else.pl ⓛ 12.00–23.00 Sun–Thur, 12.00–24.00 Fri & Sat ⓝ Tram: 1, 2, 6; Bus: 109, 409

◐ *Wrap up warm for the Zakopane winter*

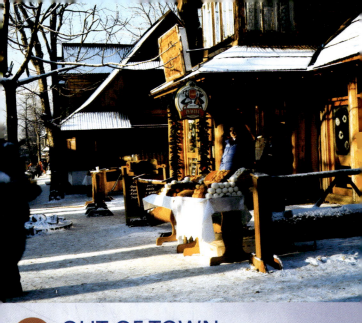

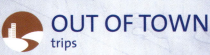

OUT OF TOWN
trips

OUT OF TOWN

Nowa Huta

On 17 May 1947 the Polish Government Presidium approved plans to construct a combined city and steelworks for 100,000 people as part of a massive project to rebuild the country at the end of World War II. The result, Nowa Huta (New Steelworks), is generally accepted to be a masterpiece of Socialist Realist architectural planning. Built 10 km (6 miles) east of central Krakow 'to enrage and humiliate the conservative and religious people of the city', Nowa Huta, far from becoming the socialist utopian dream it was meant to be, turned into one of the major hotbeds of Catholic-driven anti-communist activity during the early 1980s. Slowly reinventing itself as a tourist attraction, Nowa Huta offers an intriguing adventure both as a pilgrimage site for enthusiasts of Ostalgie and, much more surprisingly, as a place to relax in the countryside and visit one or two historical religious sites.

The Tourist Information Centre provides stacks of information on Nowa Huta, including some leaflets in English. There's a walking tour of the area that takes in the entrance to the steelworks, but concentrates mostly on the history of Kościelniki, the village that once stood here. An English translation of the route is available on the website at ⓦ www.krakow.pl, plus it's been thoughtfully signposted in both Polish and English throughout the town. A small museum on life and culture in the area can be found inside the tourist centre building.

Tourist Information Centre ⓐ Os Słoneczne 16 ⓣ 012 425 97 75 ⓦ www.mhk.pl ⓛ 10.00–14.30 Wed–Sat & 2nd Sun of the month (May–Oct); 10.30–14.00 Wed–Sat & 2nd Sun of the month (Nov–Apr) ⓘ Admission charge; free on Wed (Nov–Apr)

Welcome to Nowa Huta, centrepiece of the Socialist Realist project

OUT OF TOWN

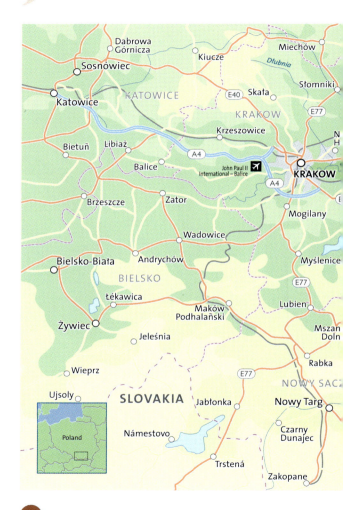

NOWA HUTA

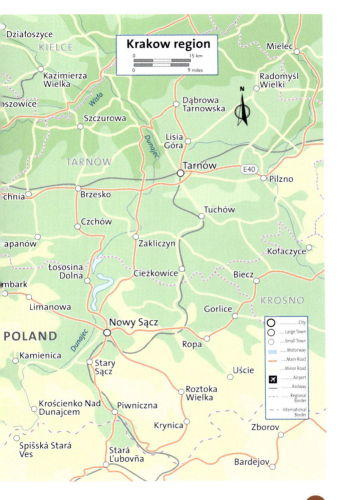

OUT OF TOWN

GETTING THERE

Trams 4 and 15 run to Nowa Huta from the city centre and take about 30 minutes to get there. Get off at the pl Centralny stop if you want to start your adventure there, or, if you feel like seeing the main Socialist Realist sights the other way round, take tram 4 all the way to the Kombinat stop outside the Administrative Centre and walk back to the centre. A daytime taxi to Nowa Huta will set you back about 30 zł.

SIGHTS & ATTRACTIONS

Arka Pana Church

Arguably the most interesting church in Krakow, the Arka Pana, or the Church of the Blessed Virgin Mary Queen of Poland (to give it its full title), was constructed with no help from the communist authorities between 1967 and 1977 to a radical design by Wojciech Pietrzyk. The estimated two million stones used for the façade were brought on-site by hand, the concrete mixed in wheelbarrows, and the whole building assembled manually in the manner of a medieval cathedral. Built on a foundation that includes a stone from the tomb of St Peter in the Vatican given to the church by the late Pope John Paul II, the two-level interior is no less inspiring. Of particular note are a tiny fragment of the mineral rutile, fixed in the tabernacle and brought all the way from the moon by the crew of *Apollo 11*, a controversial figure of Christ on the cross that shows him ready to fly to heaven, and the extraordinary *Our Lady of the Armoured Troops* sculpture made from 10 kg (22 lb) of shrapnel removed

NOWA HUTA

Arka Pana Church, built by hand by the people of Nowa Huta

OUT OF TOWN

from Polish soldiers wounded at Monte Cassino. The site of monthly protests against martial law in the early 1980s, the spectacular church is about as far removed from the average perception of Nowa Huta as it gets. A highly recommended stop. Ul Obrońców Krzyża 1, Bieńczycach 012 642 52 40 06.00–19.00 daily

Mogiła

In 1973 the boundaries of Nowa Huta changed, incorporating a number of areas of historical interest. Particularly remarkable is the small area known as Mogiła immediately east of the centre, which boasts two fine churches. The first, the **Assumption of the Virgin Mary and St Wenceslas' Church** (Ul Klasztorna 11), dates from the transition period between Romanesque and Gothic styles, is decorated with some wonderful folk paintings, and is considered to be one of the most important religious buildings in Małopolska. Across the street is Krakow's only wooden church. Built in 1466, the tiny St Bartholomew's is, unusually for Poland, built in the shape of a cross and is the only wooden church in Poland with three naves in a hall arrangement. Tram: 15 from pl Centralny east to the Klasztorna stop and head south down Ul Klasztorna

Museum of the Armed Act

An intriguing museum dedicated to the people of Nowa Huta who fought and died for their country during World War II. In Polish only, the exhibits will be lost on some, but a visit is highly recommended if not least for the extraordinary and disturbing tableaux of scenes from life in Krakow between 1939 and 1945.

NOWA HUTA

St Bartholomew's in Mogiła sits in contrast to the concrete of Nowa Huta

OUT OF TOWN

a Os Górali 23 012 644 35 17 10.00–15.00 Mon–Fri
 Admission by donation

Socialist Realist architecture
Socialist Realism was the only officially recognised art form within the Soviet Union from the 1930s until its final collapse in 1991. Supposedly capable of furthering the goals of communism, Socialist Realist art embodied everything from painting to architecture. More often than not a dismal attempt at elevating the working classes into heroes through a stifling collective creative process, Socialist Realism was exported on a global scale. Of the many Socialist Realist sights to see in Nowa Huta, the area stretching northeast from pl Centralny to the former Lenin steelworks is of most interest. The pompous and absurd Stalinist-Baroque pl Centralny (Central Square) dates from 1949, was renamed in honour of Ronald Reagan, and is currently rumoured to be awaiting a statue of Elvis Presley. Surrounded on three sides by large grey blocks that have received the full Socialist Realist treatment, five grand avenues radiate from the square, of which the partially pedestrianised al Róż to the north, where the town's statue of Lenin once stood, is perhaps the most exemplary. Along al Róż on the right is Park Ratuszowy, which, as well as offering a brief respite from the horrors of concrete, is a popular summer haunt for retired male steelworkers to sit and play cards, and gives an indication of the way the town's architects tried to blend nature, architecture and people together. A little further up, just past the Tourist Information Centre and museum, head east on ul S Żeromskiego and follow the road round to the right and on to the huge

al Solidarności (Solidarity Avenue). This brief walk takes you through a short section of leafy streets indicative of the entire town's original philosophy. Going east along al Solidarności you pass the large lake known as Zalew nad Dłubnia, the site of a big water park built as part of Nowa Huta's new, friendlier image. Immediately behind the lake is the modern Santorini Hotel (see page 113), whose restaurant is a good place to stop for something substantial to eat. The jewel in Nowa Huta's architectural crown can be found at the far eastern end of al Solidarności. The administrative centre of the Huta im Sendzimira (Sendzimir Steelworks Factory) is made up of two huge buildings that are generally believed to be Poland's best examples (after Warsaw's Palace of Culture and Science) of Socialist Realist architecture. Topped, somewhat incongruously, with all manner of Baroque swirls and fiddly details, these ghastly beasts are referred to by the locals as the 'Doges', after the grand palace in Venice which they apparently resemble.

CULTURE

Ludowy Theatre
Situated between two football fields, where gangs of punks and skinheads hang around, the renowned Ludowy (People's) Theatre is famous for bringing these two warring factions together to stage a version of *Romeo and Juliet*. With its absurd Doric columns and chandeliers, a visit to the Ludowy Theatre is worth the effort, even if you're not planning to attend a performance. ⓐ Os Teatralne 34 ⓣ 012 680 21 12 ⓞ Opening hours vary according to production

OUT OF TOWN

Norwid Cultural Centre
An unremarkable building were it not for the fact that at the top of the stairs hangs a permanent display of paintings by the 1960s avant-garde Krakow Group. Well worth a look inside. ⓐ Os Górali 5 ⓣ 012 644 27 65 ⓦ www.okn.edu.pl ⓗ 08.00–21.00 Mon–Fri, 09.00–21.00 Sat & Sun

RETAIL THERAPY

Not unlike eating in Nowa Huta (see below), shopping in the town is a cheerless event aimed almost exclusively at the local residents. An interesting way of combining the two and making the most of a bad lot is by visiting the local outdoor market. A typical affair, as found throughout Eastern Europe, the market in Nowa Huta consists almost entirely of fake designer clothing, bin liners and food. The food, however, is represented by a good choice of fresh bread, cheese, sausages, fruit and vegetables, creating the perfect opportunity to make up a picnic that can be eaten in the park.

Nowa Huta Market ⓐ Bieńczycki pl Targowy ⓣ 012 641 48 77 ⓗ 06.00–18.00 Mon–Fri, 06.00–14.00 Sat & Sun

TAKING A BREAK

Café Lura £ Inside the Ludowy Theatre. You'll hardly be writing postcards home about how great the place is, but it's not that bad either. It's a good stop for filling up on coffee and sticky buns before heading off on your next Socialist Realist adventure.

NOWA HUTA

Os Teatralne 34 012 680 21 26 1 hr before and 30 mins after performances

Cocktail Bar £ Multicoloured walls, cheap burgers, beer and average coffee. This is the Nowa Huta experience at its best. Os Centrum C 1 012 644 28 07 10.00–23.00 Mon–Fri, 11.00–23.00 Sat & Sun

AFTER DARK

Restauracja Santorini ££ If it's after dark and you're in Nowa Huta, then you're probably staying in the attached hotel (below) anyway. Featuring nice modern touches and English-speaking waiters, this is by far the best restaurant in Nowa Huta, but it's recommended you avoid the international dishes and go for something Polish. Ul Bulwarowa 35B 012 644 91 11
 10.00–23.00 daily

ACCOMMODATION

Santorini Hotel ££ Good-value three-star accommodation in a large pink building immediately west of the Zalew nad Dłubnia lake. Facilities include satellite television, minibars and Internet access. Ul Bulwarowa 35B 012 680 51 95
 www.santorinikrakow.pl

OUT OF TOWN

Zakopane

Poland's biggest fire hazard, the fabulous wooden town of Zakopane has been attracting hikers, artists and winter-sports enthusiasts since Tytus Chałubinski announced the beneficial healing properties of its climate to an unsuspecting world in 1886. Nestled inside a small valley between the jagged Tatra Mountains and the little hillside hamlet of Gubałówka 110 km (68 miles) south of Krakow, the country's unofficial winter capital, with its trademark Zakopane Style filigreed timber houses, fine skiing and fresh mountain air, offers an enticing diversion away from its mighty neighbour in the north.

Not including the mountains, Zakopane can be roughly dissected into three main areas. The compact town centre is the first natural port of call, and is the scene of the town's main action as well as where the major sights are to be found. To the north is Gubałówka, a tiny settlement on top of a hill reached by a funicular railway; there's lots to do there and it's a good place to enjoy local food and a spectacular view of the Tatras. Finally there's the skiing, which in town is pretty tame and can be found in several places around the edge of Zakopane. The serious skiing is further south and is accessed via cable car from the south of the town. Buying a map before you travel to Zakopane is recommended. The Empik Megastore (see page 135) stocks several.

Not surprisingly for a major tourist destination, Zakopane is brimming with private tourist information centres, all of which offer the same basic services and sell a few maps and small guides to the town and surrounding mountains. The official,

ZAKOPANE

◐ *The rugged Tatras rise over Zakopane*

OUT OF TOWN

◆ *Detail from the St Mary's cemetery*

state-run tourist point sells maps and local guidebooks and provides a few free brochures in English. Still relying on Polish tourists for most of its trade, Zakopane is yet to offer anywhere near the kind of English-language services you get in Krakow.

Tourist Information Centre ⓐ Ul Kościuszki 17 ⓣ 018 201 22 11 ⓦ www.promocja.zakopane.pl ⓒ 09.00–17.00 Mon–Fri & every 2nd weekend

GETTING THERE

By rail

With the likelihood of a long journey on an ancient train with no facilities and the distinct possibility of having to change trains at least once along the way, travelling by rail to Zakopane is not recommended. Zakopane's train station is next to the bus station and is even less glamorous. The only advantage of leaving bags here is that there are a number of lockers (4–8 zł), which can be accessed around the clock. Getting into town is the same as if you're arriving by bus.

By road

A regular bus service runs daily between 05.10 and 21.05 from Krakow's main bus station, taking about two hours in good weather. A one-way ticket costs 20 zł and can be bought from the driver. Depending on whether you catch a state-run or privately operated bus, you'll be dropped off either at the central bus station (with the former) or outside the Grand Hotel. Either way, the town centre is a five-minute walk west along ul Kościuszki. The bus station is a lacklustre affair, useful for its

OUT OF TOWN

toilet facilities (1.50–2 zł) and a left luggage office in the main building (🕒 07.00–19.00 ❶ 5 zł per piece). Outside these hours, use the lockers. There's an ATM outside. Taxis should be parked outside the station and will set you back about 5 zł for a ride into the town centre. Alternatively, go into the Grand Hotel a few metres west of the station and ask them to call you one.

SIGHTS & ATTRACTIONS

St Mary of Częstochowa Church
Built between 1847 and 1851 by Sebastian Gasienica Sobczak, a highlander craftsman, St Mary's is the oldest wooden church in Zakopane. The graveyard is the final resting place of many of the town's most famous sons and daughters. ⓐ Ul Kościeliska 4 🕒 06.30–19.30 daily

Tatra Museum
A fitting dedication to Zakopane's founding father Tytus Chałubinski (1820–99), this serves as a good introduction to the life and culture of the local *górale* mountain folk as well as the flora and fauna of the region. Not much in English, however. ⓐ Ul Krupówki 10 ❶ 018 201 52 05 ⓦ www.muzeumtatrzanskie.com.pl 🕒 09.00–17.00 Wed–Sat, 09.00–15.00 Sun (year-round); also open 09.00–17.00 Tues (May–Sept) ❶ Admission charge

Zakopane Style Museum at Willa Koliba
Housed inside the charming Willa Koliba (1894), this was the first house to be designed and built in the distinctive

ZAKOPANE

◆ *Distinctive folk art, Tatra Museum*

OUT OF TOWN

Zakopane Style by local resident and minor celebrity Stanisław Witkiewicz. Here you'll find a fairy-tale re-creation of how people used to live in the region at the turn of the 20th century.
ⓐ Ul Kościeliska 18 ⓣ 018 201 36 02 ⓦ www.muzeum tatrzanskie.com.pl ⓛ 09.00–17.00 Wed–Sat, 09.00–15.00 Sun
ⓘ Admission charge

THE TATRAS

A magnificent chain of peaks straddling Poland and Slovakia, the Tatras (or the High Tatras to give them their proper name) form the highest section of the Carpathians. With peaks in Poland rising to almost 2,500 m (8,200 ft), the Polish Tatras are a truly wonderful sight, featuring dense forests full of brown bears, eagles, chamois and other less notable creatures, plus large lakes and an abundance of mountain huts available for rent. A popular summertime hiking, rock-climbing and paragliding destination, the Tatras really come to life during the winter, when the Poles turn out in droves to take advantage of the good skiing, snowboarding and snowmobile adventures the mountains have to offer.

The **Tatra National Park Museum** is an indication that the West is yet to discover the Tatras – it's sadly lacking in English explanations – but it's a good place to pick up information on things to see and do in the mountains.
ⓐ Ul Chałubińskiego 42A ⓣ 018 206 32 03 ⓦ www.tpn.pl
ⓛ 08.00–16.00 Mon–Sat

Zakopane Style Museum – Inspirations
In this new museum in a 19th-century wooden house, you'll find the regional highlander architecture, arts and folk crafts that Stanisław Witkiewicz drew on to create the distinctive, idealised Zakopane Style. ⓐ Droga do Rojów 6 ⓣ 018 201 22 94 ⓦ www.muzeumtatrzanskie.com.pl ⓛ 09.00–17.00 Wed–Sat, 09.00–15.00 Sun ⓘ Admission charge

RETAIL THERAPY

If you like cheap souvenirs, you'll love Zakopane. Sometimes they threaten to overshadow the fabulous architecture in the town centre, and the temptation to buy a fake rug or hand-carved wooden spoon from one of the endless rows of identical market stalls is hard to resist. The best place to pick up a memento of your visit is in the large market at the northern end of ul Krupówki. This is also the best place in town to pick up CDs of the local folk music, which ranges in style from the sublime to the unpalatable.

Foto Koliba A good supply of disposable cameras plus accessories for digital and analogue cameras of every persuasion. ⓐ Ul Krupówki 13 & 17 ⓣ 018 206 41 82 ⓛ 09.00–20.00 daily

Galeria M Jędrysiak A small gallery and shop at the southern entrance to the market on ul Krupówki. Some quality paintings and sculptures by artists from all over the country. ⓐ Ul Droga na Gubałówka 2 ⓣ 018 201 35 46 ⓛ 12.00–17.00 daily

OUT OF TOWN

TAKING A BREAK

Almost every menu in town features a few *górale* or highlander-style, meat-heavy dishes, guaranteed to keep you at bursting point for several hours. In summer the streets offer countless opportunities to eat on the hoof, with fabulous grilled meat being sold every few metres and ladies everywhere selling *precle* and *oscypki*.

Gubałówka £ A large mountain lodge with breathtaking views of the mountains in the little settlement of the same name at the top of Zakopane's fun funicular ride, the only thing missing here is Julie Andrews. Young girls in traditional costumes bring good-value mountain food to your table while you dream about giving up the rat race and farming goats for the rest of your days. ⓐ Ul Gubałówka ⓣ 018 206 36 30 ⓛ 10.00–18.00 daily

Morskie Oko ££ A curious combination of mountain hut and canteen, complete with a grand piano, retirement-age dinner ladies and sometimes even a disco. Average-quality *żurek* and *bigos* dished out before your very eyes. Excellent if you're in a hurry, and not too bad if you're not. ⓐ Ul Krupówki 30 ⓣ 018 201 50 66 ⓦ www.morskieoko.pl ⓛ 12.00–24.00 Fri–Sun (Mar–May & Sept–Nov); 12.00–24.00 daily (June–Aug & Dec–Feb)

Grand Hotel Stamary Bar £££ Rocket-fuel espressos in the comfort of a posh hotel bar, plus food from the adjoining restaurant brought to your table if you're feeling peckish. Hardly indicative of Zakopane, but who cares? The private buses back to Krakow leave from right outside the window, making this place possibly the best waiting room in Poland. ⓐ Ul Kościuszki 19 ⓘ 018 202 45 10 ⓣ 13.00–24.00 daily

AFTER DARK

RESTAURANTS

Gazdowo Kuźnia ££ Sit inside and eat your mountain food or scrambled eggs and bacon while reclining in a sleigh, or if it's summer have one of their kebabs from the stall outside. The kebab meat in question is carved straight off a rotating pig, slipped inside a piece of hot crispy bread and garnished with salad and hot chilli mayonnaise. This alone is worth the trip to Zakopane. ⓐ Ul Krupówki 1 ⓘ 018 201 72 01 ⓦ www.gazdowo kuznia.pl ⓣ 11.00–last customer daily

BARS

Paparazzi A Polish institution, the Paparazzi chain's Zakopane outlet features its usual walls lined with iconic photographs as well as a range of quality cocktails to keep you in here until well after throwing-out time. ⓐ Ul Gen Galicy 8 ⓘ 018 206 32 51 ⓦ www.paparazzi.com.pl ⓣ 16.00–01.00 Mon–Fri, 12.00–01.00 Sat & Sun

Café Piano Zakopane's quirkiest drinking establishment features glass-topped tables full of plants, the usual array of wooden seating and, strangely, some swings by the bar. ⓐ Ul Krupówki 63 ⓘ 018 201 21 08 ⓣ 15.00–24.00 daily

OUT OF TOWN

ACCOMMODATION

A town of just 30,000, Zakopane receives around 1.5 million tourists every year. Accordingly, accommodation books up well in advance, especially during the peak winter season between Christmas and the start of March. The Tourist Information Centre (see page 117) can help you find a bed. Alternatively, depending on the condition of your wallet, try one of the two following options.

Gospoda Pod Niebem £ A dirt-cheap Gubałówka accommodation option inside a lovely wooden house. The basic but charming rooms come with simple showers and not a lot else, but the views are spectacular if you choose the right room.
ⓐ Ul Droga Stanisława Zubka 5, Gubałówka ⓣ 060 497 01 07
ⓦ www.podniebem.zakopane.pl

Grand Hotel Stamary £££ Catering to the local nouveau riche, this magnificent hotel next to the bus station offers quality rooms and top-notch service for the price of a Travelodge in Northampton. Other incentives for sleeping here include a fully equipped spa and wellness centre. ⓐ Ul Kościuszki 19
ⓣ 018 202 45 10

◗ *Wawel is particularly picturesque during winter*

PRACTICAL
information

PRACTICAL INFORMATION

Directory

GETTING THERE
By air
Krakow is served by direct flights from most major airports in Europe. Several low-cost airlines as well as the Polish national carrier, LOT, operate direct daily flights from a number of airports in the UK. Flying time from London is about two and a half hours.

Krakow Balice Airport Ul Kapitana Medweckiego 1
012 639 30 00 www.krakowairport.pl
easyJet www.easyjet.com
Jet2 www.jet2.com
LOT www.lot.com
Ryanair www.ryanair.com

Many people are aware that air travel emits CO_2, which contributes to climate change. You may be interested in the possibility of lessening the environmental impact of your flight through the charity **Climate Care** (www.jpmorganclimatecare.com), which offsets your CO_2 by funding environmental projects around the world.

By road
Before you set off in your car, be warned: Polish road fatality figures are among the worst in Europe, a result of the notoriously treacherous state of Polish roads, and the icy and snowy conditions during the winter. The bad condition of the roads in and around Krakow is being addressed, however, which will make driving much more pleasurable.

DIRECTORY

ENTRY FORMALITIES

Poland joined the Schengen system in December 2007. Arriving in the country has never been easier, although spot passport checks are still occasionally held on the land borders. Getting in and out of Belarus, Kaliningrad and Ukraine still remains problematic.

Citizens from EU countries and people from Australia, New Zealand, Canada and the United States can enter Poland without a visa and stay for a period of up to three months within any one year (six months for UK passport holders). Poland's entry into the European Union was meant to simplify duty-free allowances, but there remains an enormous amount of confusion over this issue; travellers are therefore advised to contact their local Polish embassy or consulate (see page 137) before they leave home.

TRAVEL INSURANCE

It's advisable to take out adequate travel insurance covering medical expenses, theft, loss, repatriation, personal liability and cancellation. EU citizens with a European Health Insurance Card (see 'Health, safety & crime', page 128) are still advised to have private medical insurance as well. If you're bringing your own vehicle, ensure that you have the appropriate insurance, and remember to pack the insurance documents and your driving licence. You'll need to make a police report for non-medical claims, and ensure you keep any receipts for medical treatment.

MONEY

The Polish currency is the złoty (zł), divided into 100 groszy. Exchange bureaux (*kantor*) are common and ATMs are a standard fixture throughout Krakow. Paying by credit card is getting easier, although there are still a few places in the centre that take cash only. Many places in Nowa Huta and Zakopane are yet to catch on to the pleasures of plastic. As a consequence of the world economic crisis, Poland shelved plans to join the euro in 2011 (see page 15).

HEALTH, SAFETY & CRIME

Local tap water tastes funny but is safe to drink. There's little danger of getting food poisoning while in Krakow, although you should exercise caution when eating mushrooms; picking wild ones in the autumn is very much a national pastime, and over many years Polish immune systems have built up a natural resistance to many fungi that might lose you a night's sleep if you have a sensitive stomach, or in some cases could even kill you.

Healthcare standards can be low, although there are now many smart private clinics in and around Krakow, drawing patients from all over the world for procedures from plastic surgery to dentistry. Quality healthcare comes with an almost Western price tag. All hospitals and clinics will have at least one English-speaking member of staff on duty at all times. Many chemists speak at least a little English. For more information see 'Medical services' (page 136). UK and EU citizens are entitled to reduced-cost, sometimes free, medical treatment on presentation of a valid **European Health Insurance Card** (EHIC, apply online at w www.dh.gov.uk/travellers).

Nevertheless, private medical insurance is still advised, and is essential for all non-EU visitors.

Krakow is a relatively safe city by European standards. The average Polish criminal is personified by the stereotypical image of the petty thief, who gets his kicks from preying on idiot foreigners who leave their wallets and mobile phones in unattended pockets.

OPENING HOURS

Most museums open at about 10.00, closing between 14.00 and the early evening. Monday is the traditional day for most museums to bolt their doors. Churches generally open early to allow people to pray on the way to work. Office hours follow the same pattern as the rest of Europe, but are still often punctuated with longer-than-average lunch breaks. Banks open at about 08.00 and will stay open until 18.00 in most cases, with the majority closed on weekends. Retail hours are harder to pin down, with markets opening up around the same time you're being poured into a taxi after a night out, and other shops following from about 09.00 onwards.

TOILETS

Polish toilets, often marked with a circle for women and a triangle for men, are improving, but many leave much to be desired. Several places, including decent restaurants, bus and train stations, and McDonald's (for non-customers), charge a small fee for using their toilets, usually 1.50–2 zł. There are clean public toilets in several places in the Planty; Galeria Kazimierz and Galeria Krakowska also have free toilet facilities.

PRACTICAL INFORMATION

CHILDREN
Poland is a child-friendly country that somehow manages to overlook the basic needs of children. Although there are plenty of parks and adventure playgrounds scattered around Krakow, finding baby-changing facilities, more than one high chair or a glass smaller than a bucket in most restaurants remains a fruitless task. As well as the zoo (see page 97) and water park at Nowa Huta, parents might like to let their children wind down a little at the **H Jordana Park** (ⓐ Al 3 Maja 11 Ⓝ Tram: 15, 18), which has an excellent playground as well as rowing boats and a few other things to keep the little ones occupied.

COMMUNICATIONS
Internet
For several years now, the whole of the Rynek Główny has been a free Wi-Fi zone (Ⓦ www.cracowonline.com) and the sight of tourists checking their emails while sitting on an ancient stone wall was common even before the advent of the smartphone. Internet cafés still have their uses, however.

Garinet Tucked away at the back of a narrow alleyway, find a handful of fast machines complete with Skype, plus the option of cheap international calls courtesy of a standard telephone.
ⓐ Ul Floriańska 18 ⓣ 012 423 22 33 Ⓦ www.garinet.pl
🕘 09.00–22.00 daily

Hetmańska With 20 computers, all with Internet, copying, printing and scanning facilities, and boasting an air-conditioned room for smokers, this 24-hour Internet café is handy for

DIRECTORY

TELEPHONING POLAND

To call Krakow from abroad, dial your international access code (usually 00), then the national code for Poland (48), followed by the area code for Krakow minus the initial 0 (12) then the local number. Somewhat confusingly, the prefix 012 at the start of a telephone number is both the code for Krakow and a part of the number. So, if you're calling from one Krakow landline to another, you'll need to include the 012 at the beginning. Likewise, if you're calling Krakow from another city in Poland, dial the ten-figure number starting with 012. If you're calling a landline from a Polish mobile, just dial the ten-figure number. If you're using the Plus GSM service, drop the first 0.

TELEPHONING ABROAD

To phone home from Krakow, dial the outgoing code (00), followed by the relevant country code (see below), area code (minus the initial 0 if there is one) and then the local number.

Australia 61
New Zealand 64
Republic of Ireland 353
South Africa 27
UK 44
USA & Canada 1

National enquiries ⓘ 912
International operator ⓘ 901

hostellers near the Rynek Główny. ⓐ Ul Bracka 4 ⓣ 012 430 01 08 ⏲ 24 hrs

Phones

Payphones are expensive and cards are often sold in Krakow without any credit on them. Your best option is to use one of the VOIP services available in many Internet cafés (see above) or a local SIM card. If you've got an unblocked mobile phone and you are too cheap to roam, take advantage of one of Poland's three mobile operators' prepaid services. All three companies sell SIM starter packs for less than 10 zł.

Era ⓐ Ul Wielicka 259 (Tesco) ⓣ 012 657 78 98 ⏲ 09.00–21.00 Mon–Sat, 09.00–18.00 Sun

Orange ⓐ Ul Kamieńskiego 11 ⓣ 012 422 29 59 ⏲ 10.00–21.00 daily

Plus GSM ⓐ Ul Królewska 57 ⓣ 012 396 21 50 ⏲ 10.00–18.00 Mon–Fri, 10.00–14.00 Sat

Post

The Polish postal service is reliable albeit a little slow at times, with letters and postcards often taking a week or more to reach the UK. Krakow is not short on post offices or boxes, the latter being red with a yellow post horn on a blue background. The city's Main Post Office (see below) uses a queue ticket system for everything except sending parcels (at windows 1–4) and buying stamps (windows 2–14). Letters and postcards cost 1.30 zł to send within Poland and 2.40 zł to all other destinations.

Poczta Główna (Main Post Office) ⓐ Ul Westerplatte 20 ⓣ 012 422 66 96 ⏲ 07.30–20.30 Mon–Fri, 08.00–14.00 Sat, 09.00–14.00 Sun

ELECTRICITY

Polish domestic electricity flows out of the walls at 220 V, 50 Hz, and sockets are of the round, two-pin European variety. People travelling from outside continental Europe should bring an appropriate adaptor, and US travellers will need a transformer as well.

TRAVELLERS WITH DISABILITIES

Facilities for the disabled are only just starting to appear, mostly due to the fact that EU legislation demands it. New buildings must meet rigid standards, but since one of the main reasons for visiting Krakow is to have a poke around its antiquated sights, this is little comfort. The Poles are often their own worst enemies and are in such a general state of denial over these issues that welcome additions to the city, like disabled parking spaces that the able-bodied masses consider fair game, might as well not exist at all. Getting around isn't a lot better, although all of the new bendy buses in town are equipped with disabled access as standard. To date, only tram lines 8, 34, 36 and 38 are capable of accommodating wheelchairs. The following may be of some use:

Disabled Persons Transport Advisory Committee UK
ⓦ http://dptac.independent.gov.uk

SATH (Society for Accessible Travel & Hospitality) US
ⓐ 347 Fifth Ave, Suite 605, New York, NY 10016 ⓣ 212 447 7284
ⓦ www.sath.org

TOURIST INFORMATION

The city centre is teeming with tourist information centres, both state-run and private. Remember, however, that advice from the

PRACTICAL INFORMATION

○ *Sights in the city centre are well signposted*

private ones isn't always impartial. Working for a small cash commission is an accepted way for tourist information staff to top up a modest salary. The city's official tourism website is w www.krakow.pl, and two good ports of call are:

Małopolska Tourist Information For information about the wider region, including Zakopane. a Ul Grodzka 31 t 012 421 77 06 w www.mcit.pl, www.visitmalopolska.pl ⓒ 09.00–21.00 daily (Apr–Oct); 09.00–20.00 daily (Nov–Mar)

Tourist Information Office State-run, and quite possibly the best in town. a Rynek Główny 1 (in the Town Hall Tower) t 012 433 73 10 w www.krakow.pl ⓒ 09.00–19.00 (Apr–Sept); 10.00–18.00 (Oct); 10.00–17.00 (Nov–Mar)

BACKGROUND READING

Three books worth picking up are all produced by the local publisher Wydawnictwo Bezdroża (w www.bezdroza.pl). Written by locals with a passion for the areas they cover, each one contains heaps of valuable insights into (and strange stories behind) the people, buildings and events that have shaped Krakow. Individual guidebooks in their own right, complete with walking tours, information on bars and restaurants and some great colour photography, the series also provides the necessary background reading that the vast majority of other locally published books overlook. Sadly lacking in detail in just one or two areas, the well-translated, pocket-size books cost around 35 zł each in the Empik Megastore (see below).

Krakow's Kazimierz by Agnieszka Legutko-Ołownia. A brilliant evocation of Krakow's former Jewish quarter and rapidly up-and-coming bohemian district. Essential reading for anyone with a special interest in Kazimierz.

Krakow's Nowa Huta by Maciej Miezian. The first book in English to break away from the obsession with Nowa Huta's communist past. Pages and pages of magnificent and often hilarious insights, with tours of the hitherto unpublished rural parts of Nowa Huta.

Krakow's Old Town by Maciej Miezian. Verging on a masterpiece, this book covers anything and everything you ever wanted to know about the old town and Wawel. Old-town sights as well as stories about alchemists, butchers and a very faithful dog called Dżok (Jock).

Empik Megastore Along with the above-mentioned books, Empik's flagship Krakow store stocks a huge selection of CDs, DVDs, maps, guidebooks and some English-language paperbacks.
ⓐ Rynek Główny 5 ☏ 012 429 41 62 ⏱ 09.00–22.00

PRACTICAL INFORMATION

Emergencies

EMERGENCY NUMBERS
Ambulance ❶ 999
Fire ❶ 998
Police ❶ 997

It's unlikely anyone at the other end of the three numbers listed above will speak English. However, the Polish police now operate a daytime and evening emergency call centre for foreigners in English and German that closes around the time you'll probably need it (🕒 08.00–24.00): from a local landline, call ❶ 0800 20 03 00 and if roaming, call ❶ +48 22 601 55 55

MEDICAL SERVICES
Krakowskie Pogotowie Ratunkowe (Krakow Emergency Ambulance Service) English-speaking medical services for emergencies, just east of the city centre. ⓐ Ul św Łazarza 14 ❶ 012 424 42 00 (from a fixed-line telephone) ❶ 112 (from a mobile phone) 🕒 24 hrs

Chemist
Apteka ⓐ Ul Kalwaryjska 94 ❶ 012 656 18 50 🕒 24 hrs

Dentists
Dent America ⓐ Pl Szczepański 3 ❶ 012 421 89 48 ⓦ www.dentamerica.pl 🕒 08.30–20.00 Mon–Fri, 08.30–14.00 Sat
Denta-Med ⓐ Ul Na Zjeździe 13 ❶ 012 259 80 00 🕒 24 hrs

EMERGENCIES

> **EMERGENCY PHRASES**
>
> | Help! | Fire! | Stop! |
> |---|---|---|
> | Pomocy! | Pożar! | Stop! |
> | *Po-mo-ste!* | *Po-jar!* | *Stop!* |
>
> **Call an ambulance/a doctor/the police/the fire service!**
> Wezwać pogotowie/lekarza/policję/straż pożarna!
> *Ve-zvach po-go-toh-vyeh/le-ka-jah/po-lee-tsyeh/straj po-jar-nom!*

POLICE
Old Town Central Police Station ⓐ Rynek Główny 29 ⓣ 012 615 73 17 ⓗ 24 hrs

EMBASSIES & CONSULATES
Australia ⓐ 3rd Floor, Nautilus Building, Ul Nowogrodzka 11, Warsaw ⓣ 022 521 34 44 ⓦ www.australia.pl
Canada ⓐ Ul Matejki 1/5, Warsaw ⓣ 022 584 31 00
ⓦ www.canadainternational.gc.ca
New Zealand ⓐ Al Ujazdowskie 51, Warsaw ⓣ 022 521 05 00
ⓦ www.nzembassy.com
Republic of Ireland ⓐ Ul Mysia 5, Warsaw ⓣ 022 849 66 33
South Africa ⓐ Ul Koszykowa 54, Warsaw ⓣ 022 625 62 28
ⓦ www.gcis.gov.za
UK ⓐ Ul św Anny 9, Krakow ⓣ 012 421 70 30
ⓦ http://ukinpoland.fco.gov.uk
USA ⓐ Ul Stolarska 9, Krakow ⓣ 012 424 51 00
ⓦ http://krakow.usconsulate.gov

INDEX

A

accommodation 35–9
  Nowa Huta 113
  Zakopane 124
air travel 48, 126
alcohol 22, 27
annual events 8–11
aquarium 46
Archaeology Museum 46
Archdiocesan Museum 58
architecture 102, 110–11
Arka Pana Church 106–8
arts *see* culture
Assumption of the Virgin
  Mary and St Wenceslas'
  Church 108

B

background reading
  134–5
Barbican 58
bars, clubs & pubs
  see nightlife
Botanic Gardens 95–6
Bractwo Kurkowe 89
bread 25–6
Brotherhood of Fowlers
  89
Burgher Museum 59
bus travel 49, 117

C

cafés
  Further afield 98
  Kazimierz 83–4
  Nowa Huta 112–13
  Old town & Wawel 72–3
  Zakopane 122–3
car hire 56
Cathedral 70
Cathedral Museum 67–8
Catholicism 16
Celestat 89, 92
children 130
cinema 31
City Engineering
  Museum 81
climate 8
Cloth Hall 59, 62
concessions 44
crime 128–9
culture 12–13, 18–20, 44
customs & duty 127
cycling 32
Czartoryski Museum 62

D

disabilities 133
driving 56, 126

E

electricity 133
embassies 137
emergencies 136–7
entertainment 29–31
  see also nightlife
Ethnographical
  Museum 81
events 8–13
extreme sports 32

F

Fabryka Oskara
  Schindlera 92
festivals 8–13
food & drink 25–8, 128
football 32

G

Galeria Ora 71
Galicia Jewish Museum
  76
golf 34
Grunwald Monument 89
Gubałówka 114

H

H Jordana Park 130
health 128–9, 136
hiking 120
Hippolit House 59
Historical Museum
  of Krakow 62–3
history 14–15, 89, 95
History of Photography
  Museum 96
hotels
  see accommodation
Huta im Sendzimira 111

I

insurance 127, 128–9
Internet 130, 132
Isaac's Synagogue 76–7

J

Jagiellonian University
  Museum 63

INDEX

Jewish Cultural Centre 82–3
Jewish Festival of Culture 12–13
Jewish Krakow 12–13, 76–81, 82–3, 92, 94–5
John Paul II 15, 16, 58
Juliusz Słowacki Theatre 71

K

Kazimierz 44–5, 76–87
Kościuszko Mound 96–7
Krakow Aquarium 46
Krakow card 44
Krakow Zoo 97

L

language 24, 28, 53, 137, 144
Leonardo da Vinci 62
lifestyle 16–17
Lost Wawel 68
Ludowy Theatre 111

M

malls 22–4
Manggha Centre 92–3
markets 22, 45, 63, 82, 112, 121
Mogiła 108
money 128
Museum of the Armed Act 108, 110
Museum of National Remembrance 94–5
music 18, 29–31

N

National Museum of Art 98
nightlife 29–31
 Further afield 99–100
 Kazimierz 84–7
 Nowa Huta 113
 Old town & Wawel 73–5
 Zakopane 123
Norwid Cultural Centre 112
Nowa Huta 102

O

Old Synagogue 77
old town 58–75
opening hours 129
Oracewicz, Marcin 89
Oriental Art 68
Oskar Schindler Factory 92

P

paragliding 120
Park Ratuszowy 110
parks & green spaces 70, 95–6, 97, 110, 120, 130
passports & visas 127
Pauline Church 81–2
Pharmacy Museum 47
phones 131, 132
picnics 25, 70
pierogi 10, 25
Plac Nowy 82
Planty 70

Płaszów Concentration Camp 94
Podgórze 95
police 137
Polish Aviation Museum 96
Pope John Paul II 15, 16, 58
post 132
public holidays 11
public transport 48–9, 52–5, 106, 117

R

rail travel 49, 117
Remuh Synagogue & Cemetery 80–81
restaurants 25, 27
 Further afield 99
 Kazimierz 84–6
 Old town & Wawel 72–4
 Zakopane 122–3
rock climbing 120
Royal Castle 67
Royal Apartments 68–9
Rynek Główny 63
Rynek Underground 64

S

safety 49, 128–9, 136–7
St Bartholomew's Church 108
St Francis's Basilica 64
St Mary of Częstochowa Church 118
St Mary's Basilica 64–6

139

INDEX

SS Peter & Paul's Church 66–7
Schindler, Oskar 92
seasons 8
Sendzimir Steelworks Factory 111
shopping 22–4, 44–5, 135
  Kazimierz 83
  Nowa Huta 112
  Old town & Wawel 71–2
  Zakopane 121
skating 34
skiing 114
Socialist Realism 102, 110–11
sport & activities 32–4, 114, 120
Stare Miasto 58–75
State Rooms 68–9
swimming 34
symbols 4

T
Tatra Museum 118
Tatra National Park Museum 120
Tatras mountains 120
taxis 56, 106
theatre 18, 31, 71, 111
tickets 31
time difference 48
tipping 27
toilets 129
tourist information 102, 114, 117, 133–4
tours 45, 102
trams 52–3, 106
travel insurance 127
Treasury & Armoury 70

U
UNESCO 58

W
walking 45, 102, 110–11, 120
Wawel 58–75
Wawel Cathedral 67–8, 70
Wawel Dragon 66
Wawel Hill 67–70
Wawel Hill cave 66
weather 8, 46–7
winter sports 34, 114, 120
Wyspiański, Stanisław 18, 20, 64, 70–71, 81–2
Wyspiański Museum 70–71

Z
Zakopane 114–24
Zakopane Style Museum 118–21
Zalew nad Dłubia 111
zoo 97

NOTES

ACKNOWLEDGEMENTS & FEEDBACK

ACKNOWLEDGEMENTS
Thomas Cook Publishing wishes to thank the photographers, picture libraries and other organisations, to whom the copyright belongs, for the photographs in this book.

Giacomo Bassi, page 17; Dreamstime, pages 5 (Julietphotography), 40–41 (Leesniderphotoimages), 65 (Gelia), 97 (Pryzmat), 125 (Taleksej); Krzysztof Gebarowski, page 115; Paul Thompson Images/Alamy, page 33; Pepe Rosso Restaurant, page 85; Polish National Tourist Office in London, pages 21, 37, 57, 101; Restauracja Wierzynek, page 74; Visit Poland, page 23; Richard Schofield, all others.

Project editor: Ed Robinson
Layout: Trevor Double
Proofreaders: Karolin Thomas & Kate Taylor

Send your thoughts to
books@thomascook.com

- **Found a great bar, club, shop or must-see sight that we don't feature?**
- **Like to tip us off about any information that needs a little updating?**
- **Want to tell us what you love about this handy little guidebook and more importantly how we can make it even handier?**

Then here's your chance to tell all! Send us ideas, discoveries and recommendations today and then look out for your valuable input in the next edition of this title.

Email the above address (stating the title) or write to:
pocket guides Series Editor, Thomas Cook Publishing, PO Box 227, Coningsby Road, Peterborough PE3 8SB, UK.

WHAT'S IN YOUR GUIDEBOOK?

Independent authors Impartial up-to-date information from our travel experts who meticulously source local knowledge.

Experience Thomas Cook's 165 years in the travel industry and guidebook publishing enriches every word with expertise you can trust.

Travel know-how Thomas Cook has thousands of staff working around the globe, all living and breathing travel.

Editors Travel-publishing professionals, pulling everything together to craft a perfect blend of words, pictures, maps and design.

You, the traveller We deliver a practical, no-nonsense approach to information, geared to how you really use it.

ABOUT THE AUTHOR

Based in Lithuania and the Balkans, Richard 'Sco' Schofield has been writing about and taking photographs of the more exotic parts of Europe for almost a decade. Having started his travel-writing career in Cuba, Sco now runs a travel-publishing business with two colleagues in Tirana and is a regular contributor at the European city guide publisher In Your Pocket. Most recently, he co-authored Thomas Cook's *travellers guide Albania*.

Useful phrases

English	Polish	Approx pronunciation
BASICS		
Yes	Tak	Tak
No	Nie	Nyair
Please	Proszę	Pro-sheh
Thank you	Dziękuję	Jen-koo-yair
Hello	Cześć	Cheshch
Goodbye	Do widzenia	Do vee-je-nyah
Excuse me	Przepraszam	Pshe-pra-sham
Sorry	Przepraszam	Pshe-pra-sham
That's okay	To jest O.K.	Toh yest O.K.
I don't understand	Nie rozumiem	Nyeah ro-zoo-myem
Do you speak English?	Czy mówi pan/pani po angielsku?	Che moo-vee pan/pa-nee poe an-gyels-koo?
Good morning	Dzień dobry	Jeny do-bri
Good afternoon	Dobry wieczór	Do-bri vie-choor
Good evening	Dobry wieczór	Do-bri vie-choor
Goodnight	Dobranoc	Do-bra-nots
My name is ...	Nazywam się ...	Nazyvam shiem ...
NUMBERS		
One	Jeden	Ye-den
Two	Dwa	Dva
Three	Trzy	Tshe
Four	Cztery	Chte-ri
Five	Pięć	Pyench
Six	Sześć	Shesch
Seven	Siedem	She-dem
Eight	Osiem	O-shem
Nine	Dziewięć	Je-vyench
Ten	Dziesięć	Je-shench
Twenty	Dwadzieścia	Dva-je-schchar
Fifty	Pięćdziesiąt	Peeyent-je-shont
One hundred	Sto	Sto
SIGNS & NOTICES		
Airport	Port lotniczy	Port lo-tnee-che
Rail station	Dworzec kolejowy	Dvo-zhets ko-le-yo-vi
Platform	Peron	Perron
Smoking/	Dla palących/	Dla pa-lon-tse-h/
No smoking	Dla niepalących	Dla nyair pa-lon-tse-h
Toilets	Toalety	Toe-a-lair-te
Ladies/Gentlemen	Damska/Męska	Dam-skah/Men-skah